CARE and REPAIR of ANTIQUES

by

THOMAS H. ORMSBEE

Illustrated

D1447406

GRAMERCY PUBLISHING COMPANY

NEW YORK

To the Rev. Arthur W. Hargate, D.D.

FOREWORD

During several years of lecturing in widely separated cities and by queries from readers of a syndicated series of brief articles, I have met or been in correspondence with many people, all interested in American antiques. "How can I tell if it is an antique?" "How can I know its age and where it was made?" These are the questions that have been asked me more times than any others. So, in writing this book about the selection, repair and proper care of antiques, I have kept these questions to the forefront. I have endeavored to give the chief points for individual pieces, from furniture through prints, by which a reader may judge the merits and demerits of an antique he may possess or is considering buying.

This advice does not concern those who have been collecting for some time. By trial and error, they have presumably learned about antiques the hard way and have come to have their own standards, by which they now judge additions to their collections. Of course, this experience has cost such veterans time and money. Not that there is any sure way that I know of by which this can be short-circuited. If there were, it would take much of the fun out of collecting antiques. On the other hand, with some fairly simple guides the beginner can avoid some of the more obvious pitfalls.

This is the purpose of Part One. In the case of furniture particularly, I have told of the repairs that must be made with a large proportion of pieces before they are presentable and usable in the collector's home. Such repairs are necessary and legitimate, for without the work of skillful repairmen to correct the damage of time and use there would be much less antique furniture available. Repairing is a bad thing only when a repaired piece is offered as entirely original, or when by deliberate addition of decorative detail a simple piece is made to look as if it were much finer and more sophisticated.

That is known as "glorification," and it is never justified. In about the same class is the "rebuilt" piece, in which parts of a wreck or two, plus some new wood, are assembled into what at first glance seems to be an antique.

To guard the reader against such illegitimate, overly restored pieces, I have tried to give the main points by which such things may be recognized for what they are. From long acquaintance with many antique dealers, I know that most of them dislike such pseudo-antiques and do not knowingly have one for sale, but sometimes even experienced dealers make honest mistakes. So collectors and dealers alike must be constantly alert.

In Part Two, in discussing the repairs which the collector can do for himself, I have described only the simpler ones—those that I know from personal experience can be done by almost anyone with a reasonable amount of mechanical dexterity and an average assortment of tools. If the home worker finds that he has a genuine flair for restoring ailing antiques, he can go on from there to more difficult things. But for most collectors, home repairing of antiques had better stop with the simpler projects. For major operations, it is usually the part of wisdom to call in the professional repairman. This is especially true with antique silver, china and glass. I remember to my sorrow two or three fine pieces that I damaged, not to say ruined, by my blundering attempts to repair them. With such antiques my rigid rule now is: "Don't fool around with home remedies; take it to a specialist."

T. H. O.

CONTENTS

Foreword

ILLUSTRATIONS

CHAPTER I

The Look of the Antique

"The collector or dealer who hasn't bought a phony antique thinking it was genuine doesn't live," said a dealer with a national reputation for handling antiques of the finest quality. "I've been buying in this country and in England for better than twenty-five years, but I still get fooled once in a while. Usually it is when I haven't taken time to examine a piece carefully enough. At a quick glance it seems perfect, and I get in a hurry and buy it. But then, if it happens to be furniture, my repairman has a good time setting me right when the piece reaches his shop. He puts such a blunder aside and waits to show me each wrong detail—the new leg, the inlay that has been added, the modern tool marks in a drawer bottom, all are pointed out with ill-concealed delight.

"But he's not the only one who has fun with me when I make a wrong buy. Some time ago I went to a country auction down in South Jersey. The auctioneer was already selling when I arrived, and an interesting animal-shaped bottle was up. It looked good and I bid it in for about five dollars. When my son saw it he recognized it as the kind in which a well-known imported liqueur is sold and told me that the purchase was no credit to me, either as a dealer or as a drinking man. He keeps it on a shelf in the office just to remind me that I don't know it all."

This dealer spoke from long experience. With antiques, nothing is so true as the old proverb about acting in haste and repenting at leisure. But with even the beginning collector, care and thorough examination before making a

1

purchase can go a long way toward keeping the number of fake or questionable antiques that he buys few and far between. If he has laid a good groundwork by frequent visits to museums, antiques shows and dealers' shops, and has been a good observer, his eye and mind will have become so trained that subconsciously he will recognize an antique when he sees it. In about the same way too, he will be wary of a deliberate fake or a piece of doubtful antecedents.

Unwittingly he will have developed a sixth sense, similar to that of the private detective in a metropolitan hotel who, watching hundreds of guests, spots the questionable one almost as soon as his eyes light on him. "I don't know just how we do it," such a detective once told me, "but there is something about the 'skip,' the cardsharper or other crook that warns us practically at a glance."

Antiques being mostly individual pieces with few exact duplicates, each collector must be his own sleuth. In fact, developing the ability to spot the genuine and detect the spurious is part of the fun of being a collector. If the surroundings where an interesting antique is found are not in keeping with its quality, so much the better.

A half-round Sheraton card table of cherry that I still own was one of my early lucky strikes. I first saw it about thirty years ago while riding on the rear platform of a Brooklyn trolly car. A colored porter had it perched on his shoulder and was carrying it into a second-hand furniture store. I got off the street car at the next corner and was in the store almost as soon as the table was. After a pretense of looking around, I evinced a mild interest in the newly arrived piece, found the price was five dollars and began looking it over in earnest. Turned upside down, it showed no traces of later replacements, either as to legs or part of the double top. One couldn't be certain of the wood because of the numerous coats of stain and varnish, but I bought it anyway. Subsequently I had it refinished by an expert cabinetmaker who was able to remove the layers of varnish without disturbing the patina of old cherry. Even now, whenever I look at it, there comes a warm sense of satisfaction—with the table because of its mellow glow and graceful lines, and with myself because I had sense enough to buy it.

Even before the table episode I had learned something about furniture, which was my first love among antiques, by haunting antique shops and trudging through museum galleries. I had learned that old wood has a different look from new; that any piece of furniture that has been in daily use for three generations or more is bound to bear signs of wear. These things, as well as the material from which it was made and the indications of use, not abuse, are the cardinal points that the collector first observes with any antique.

There is a difference in the material from which modern machine-made household pieces are made and that used four or more generations ago. Learning to recognize it is not too difficult, nor does it require an extensive collection at the start. Take just one antique. It may be a simple slat-back chair, a porcelain or earthenware plate, a silver spoon, a brass candlestick, or a piece of either blown or pressed glass. Put it beside a similar modern piece and compare the two. Go over them with a strong reading glass and note the difference in texture. Study them right side up and upside down. If the objects are glass, tap each lightly with a pencil. Listen for the bell-like ring of old lead glass, and the dull thud of the cheaper and later lime glass.

As I write, I have before me two blue and white plates. They were both made in one or another of the Staffordshire potteries of England. The indigo-blue tint of the transfer-printed allover decoration is about the same in each, but one plate was made for the American market fully seventy-five years earlier than the other. How does one know? The older plate has a pronounced upward curve and a slightly scalloped edge. The new plate is much flatter, and was obviously machine-pressed. Also, when I hold both plates in my hands and compare their weight, I sense that the newer one is heavier. The older a piece of Staffordshire pottery, the lighter is its comparative weight.

Next, in passing my hand lightly over both plates, my fingertips tell me that the glaze on the newer one is smoother and more glasslike. Then, by looking across both plates toward the light, I see on the older one a multitude of fine scratches caused by knife strokes in cutting meat during the countless times it saw use as a dinner plate. Also, near the center and along the inner edge of the rim the glaze is dulled, even nearly worn through as a result of the plate being piled with others like it on a cupboard shelf.

Turning the plates over, I can see that the glaze of the older is distinctly crazed and covered with a minute irregular network of light brown hair lines. This crazing was caused chiefly by repeated warmings in brick ovens or in those wood-burning cook stoves that came into use in American homes about 1825. The newer plate, never much used, has none of this crazing, the mark of age and plenty of use. Also, at three places equidistant around the rim of the antique piece, there are three groups of pinhead-like roughnesses in the glaze. The old method was to separate plates stacked in the kiln for firing with little pin-like bits of clay called *stilts*. Such stilt marks are, of course, absent in the new plate.

Lastly, there are the potter's marks. On the older plate it is impressed, and reads: "Clewes Patented Staffordshire." On the newer, the mark is printed beneath the glaze in the same blue as the design, and reads: "Wedgwood, Etruria, England." This statement of the country of origin is the result of a law passed in 1892 requiring that all merchandise imported into the United States be so marked. The newer plate is therefore proved to have been made at some date after 1892 and is consequently not to be classed as an antique. As for the plate with the Clewes mark, reference to a standard book on Staffordshire pottery discloses that James and Ralph Clewes operated their pottery at Burslem from 1819 to 1836.

I have given this step-by-step account of examining these plates so that I might show what can be learned by comparison and because I believe that careful observation is the only way by which the collector can know what he is looking for. Sometimes, when you know what to observe, it is as easy as it was with these plates; at other times, the telling points may be more difficult to find. Always, difference in the material, ways in which the work was done and what I like to call normal signs of wear can be detected if one will look hard enough. Of course, there are the rare exceptions of old pieces that were never used and were always kept scrupulously protected; but even they serve to prove the general rule that an antique will give up its clues if you will study it as carefully as you would examine the records of stocks or bonds you consider acquiring for investment.

As an example of how this side-by-side comparison of a known antique and a similar object that is comparatively new works with furniture, let us consider two bedside tables. One is of the sort that can be found in many antique shops. It has a square top, four square tapering legs and a shallow drawer in the bed. The other is part of a modern factory-made bedroom set. The finish of the antique table has the mellow tone of age. The top is somewhat scratched, and the edges of the legs, especially near the floor, are just a little battered and rounded where they have been hit by cleaning utensils in weekly cleanings over a century or more of use.

The finish of the new table is much brighter; the varnish shines; the legs are not yet much marred by use. The top still retains a certain smooth, mirror-like quality and its edges and corners are sharp. Next we examine both drawers.

Sides, back and bottom of the drawer in the antique table are of a soft wood that has taken on a light brown color, which has a slightly weathered tone because the interior was never varnished or shellacked. The drawer interior in the new table looks almost as fresh as when it left the factory, since it was as thoroughly varnished as the rest of the piece.

Look at the side pieces of the drawer from the old table. About a quarter of an inch of the lower edge of each is worn away as a result of the numberless times the drawer has been opened and shut; the drawer sides of the new table are not worn, because of less use. Finally, notice the bottom boards of both drawers. The antique one has rough planing on its underside, leaving ridges and hollows that can be felt if you pass your fingertips over it lightly. That of the new drawer is as perfectly planed on its under side as on the top. Besides, it is a piece of plywood, something never used by the old furniture makers.

The legs of the old table are joined by mortise and tenon joints to the cross members that form the bed; the legs of the new one are held in place by iron screws that pass through diagonal corner blocks concealed beneath the top. Unscrew one and you can lift that leg out of its position, which cannot be done with the legs of an old table, since its mortise and tenon joints were made fast with hot glue.

One more striking variation has to do with the quantity of wood used. Much less went into the parts of the new table than into the old. The legs are slighter, the top thinner by at least a quarter of an inch and just enough wood was used in the drawer parts to hold it together. There was no such skimping on wood with the old table, and it was made far stronger than was actually necessary.

When the old craftsmen worked, lumber was relatively cheap and they used as much as they felt was needed. Today lumber is expensive, and furniture factories naturally keep the amount of wood used as near the minimum as possible, even though the result is furniture that is too slightly built. Whether a piece will last is a question not considered.

Turning once more to my own modest collection, there is a set of Irish cut-glass decanters which date back to about 1835, and from their shape and style of cutting could easily be some twenty-five years older. These four decanters must have been treated tenderly and used only on important occasions, for they are free of chips or nicks. Visible proof of age is to be found, though, on the base of each. It consists in a myriad of fine scratches caused by fine particles of grit which gradually left their marks when the decanters were moved about.

In examining any antique, the collector will be wise to look it over in a clear light. Personally, I prefer either bright sunlight, a cold north light, or an unshaded 300- to 500-watt electric lamp. Do not be in too much of a hurry. Take time enough to get a general impression of the object. Consider the decorative details. They should jibe with the general design and construction; otherwise you are perhaps looking at a transitional piece made in an earlier style period, with decorative detail of some ten or even fifty years later.

An example of this might be an American Chippendale slant-top desk with a spread eagle inlaid in the center of the lid. This could be proper if the piece was the work of a country cabinetmaker. Many of these craftsmen continued certain designs for some time after they had gone out of favor in larger centers. Shift to newer modes was gradual, with decorative touches coming first. Such a cabinetmaker might make a Chippendale desk as late as 1790 to which he added the Hepplewhite decoration of an eagle in inlay. However, if done fairly recently by some ill-informed repairman, it would be an example of bad glorification not hard to detect, since he would use a stock inlay.

Also, since the most desirable antiques are those in mint condition—that is, as nearly perfect as when they came from the hands of their makers—one that has been repaired is naturally not as valuable. For instance, an Oriental Lowe-stoft plate that has been broken and mended so skillfully that the repair is not apparent until the plate is turned over and the rivets seen may be quite usable, but its value is only half that of the same plate in perfect condition.

Also, a mirror with regilded frame is not as desirable as one in original condition, even though the frame of the latter may have some dull spots. Old mirror glass usually has fine spots where the quicksilver is discolored, and the general tint of the silvering has a steel-like quality. Therefore a glass lacking these characteristics is probably a replacement.

There is a sheen to old silver and pewter that only age and repeated polishings over a period of years can give. New pieces in either of these metals have a totally different look. Examined under a microscope, the surface of the old pieces will show a mat of minute scratches and sometimes equally small dents. These, again, are the signs of normal wear that bespeak the genuineness of the pieces that bear them.

CHAPTER II

Where to Find Antiques

We were sitting around the hotel lobby in a small city located in the heart of the Pennsylvania Dutch country. It was late in the evening, and an antiques show being held there had closed for the day. In the group were two dealers who had booths at the show, several others who had come to buy, and two or three veteran collectors.

The usual trade gossip was going on. How "Dick," who thought he was a pretty smart fellow, had fallen for a cleverly done piece of furniture that had been glorified with added carving and inlay. The clean-up another dealer had made on a fine but not widely known pewter collection he had bought when nobody else knew it was for sale. The unusually high prices paid at a recent country auction, rivaling those of shops along New York's East 57th Street. Comments of warning about some of the newer glass and china fakes that were being peddled, and detailed descriptions of a pair of light-fingered elderly women who were adept at lifting such small but expensive antiques as Sandwich glass paperweights, choice eighteenth-century American silver, diamond-quilted Stiegel glass and signed and dated samplers.

Gradually the talk shifted to that most favored of all subjects with collectors and dealers: where to find antiques. Each had his own special anecdote. A comb-back Windsor armchair bought direct from a Negro junk dealer's Ford truck on Seventh Avenue in the heart of Harlem. An early mold-blown Zanesville glass sugar bowl, complete with domed cover, found in a bus-terminal lunchroom out in Indiana, where it was being used as a toothpick holder. A

9

Hepplewhite sideboard that had fallen to the low estate of a hen roost on a North Carolina farm. A set of wrought-iron cooking utensils and implements for the old kitchen fireplace of a Connecticut farmhouse, found safe behind the fireboard, which had not been removed for over a generation. The colored glass dolphin candlesticks bought for a fraction of their value at an auction gallery in New York City one afternoon when a bad blizzard had tied up traffic. Finally, there was the delicate candlestand of Salem craftsmanship that a young Junior Leaguer brought to a city dealer's shop direct from the warehouse where a roomful of family possessions was stored—she had tripped over the tripod legs of this piece and ruined a pair of nylons that afternoon when she went there to get a costume for the little theater play in which she had a part.

These were stories of dramatic finds, but I knew the bulk of antiques in their shops had been acquired far more prosaically. So as the group broke up I induced one of them to talk at length about how he ran his business. He is a large city dealer with over twenty-five years' experience in buying and selling antiques. His shop, a building of red brick with marble trim, was once a handsome city residence. Now, from basement to top floor, the rooms are well filled with American antiques of all sorts and periods, from the late seventeenth to early nineteenth centuries, and he has sold many fine pieces to leading collectors and important museums, especially examples of the work of Pennsylvania Dutch craftsmen and folk artists.

"Where do you find the antiques in your shop?" I asked "Little Joe," as he is known among the dealers because of his bantam size.

"Honestly, I never know where or how I'll buy my next good antique—the kind of thing I'd want to show to important collectors or museums. I just keep hunting, in the city or out in the country. I make a dozen house calls and get nothing. I'm polite to twice as many more people who come into my shop just to see what I have that is like theirs. I could get disgusted and quit going out or showing people around, but if I did I'd surely miss something worth while. I keep track of the auctions and am friendly with country dealers. I've bought a good many of my antiques from both sources. The bank roll I always have with me helps a lot too. Word has got around that I'm ready to pay spot cash for what I want, and money talks a good deal louder than a check, especially at five or six o'clock in the afternoon.

"Sure, I go out into the country whenever I've the chance to get away from the shop, Little Joe continued, "for I'm crazy about both trout fishing and hunting antiques, but I'm not telling where I go for either. One is a personal, the other a business secret. I will say this much, if a dealer doesn't get a kick out of driving a couple of hundred miles hunting for antiques, he'd better get into some other kind of business. Also, to be successful, he's got to have a good eye and be able to spot nice things without wasting too much time, and pass up what isn't so good the same way. Otherwise his shop will soon be loaded down with junk. Then the good collectors won't come around any more. They don't like to waste their time looking at a lot of ordinary things.

"At the same time, just often enough to prove that it can happen, some beginner, either a collector or dealer, picks up a really fine antique in a most unlikely place for a low price. He doesn't always know how good it is, but he feels it's not just run of the mine stuff. I have had many such things shown me. I make a point of always telling the finder what he has, for two reasons. If he's a collector, such a discovery puts him just that much further ahead and in time he'll want more and better antiques. I may be able to sell him something. If the finder is just getting started as a dealer, I tell him just what he has and make as good an offer as I can for it. He is then apt to bring other pieces to me and I have developed another good source of stock.

"Of course, there are those who bring me poor antiques, late stuff or just junk, and start arguing with me when I tell them what they have. But that's part of the antiques business. You've got to expect about so much of that. On the other hand, if they really want to know what's wrong with what they are showing me, I try to show them the difference. I even get out something of my own and compare it with what has been brought in. In my time I've started quite a few collectors and dealers by such demonstrations. It is missionary work for the good of antiques collecting. I haven't forgotten the old collector who was my teacher-customer when I first started. I used to put a new buy away and wait to show it to him. Once, after telling me what I had and in what books I might find a similar piece pictured and described, he offered to buy it. After that I had a lot more confidence. 'Joe, you've the eye to spot good antiques,' I said to myself. 'Now read and go look at what's in the museum, for the best luck in finding things won't do you any good if you don't know quality.'

"I started learning and I haven't stopped yet—don't ever expect to—and I'm always ready to listen to anybody who can tell me something new about American antiques. For in stance, quite a few years ago, near Bridgeton, New Jersey, I came across a retired glass blower, a man about seventy-five years old. He was living all by himself in a little house on a back road. I had heard he had a lily-pad pitcher. He wouldn't sell it, but I kept calling on him whenever I was down that way. One day he took me out to a shed back of his house, showed me his blower's tools and began to talk. He described each step in blowing and shaping a piece of glass, illustrating most of them with the tools used. I was fascinated. Later I had a bowl, blown of greenish bottle glass, that puzzled me. It looked good, and seemed as if it might be a real find in early Wistar glass. I took it to him. Before he was through looking it over, I had had a wonderful lesson in judging glass for quality, texture and color. He even showed me the marks, right in the glass itself, of pincer-like tools with which the rim of that bowl was folded over when it was being shaped. What success I've had in glass goes back to that old boy. I finally got his pitcher too, but not until after he was dead. I bought it from a neighbor who looked after him at the last. He'd given it to her. Now it's in my private collection to remind me of how I learned just a little more about glass."

On other occasions than at this hotel lobby gathering, I have talked with many different kinds of people about finding antiques. Some were collectors, some museum curators, and many more were dealers in various sections of the country. Also, I have had my own varied experiences, dating back to my school years in Brooklyn and summers spent in Vermont and rural Connecticut. Only last winter, in an Iowa city known for its fine ham and bacon, I was shown a collection of glass paperweights.

"Where did you get all these varieties?" was my instinctive inquiry as I scanned the sizable cabinet in which their owner kept them.

"The first half-dozen or so I got from the man at our local rubbish dump," she replied with some pride. "He raked them out of the loads of household refuse and I paid him half a dollar each for them. At that time I didn't know anything about paperweights, but they were pretty and I wanted more. So on vacations or on other trips I was always looking. Occasionally I'd find one in a country dealer's shop. Others I spotted in various cities. As my collection grew, a few friends and relatives gave me weights that had been in their families.

"One time on a convention trip with my husband I saw a newspaper story about a loan exhibition at the Chicago Art Institute. On our way home we had a day in Chicago and I spent most of it at the Institute, looking at the weights displayed and taking notes on what the labels said. After that I was really a paperweight collector. I read everything I could find that had been written about them. I began writing to various dealers who advertised weights. Now and then I bought one this way and I swapped my duplicates. There are still many other weights I need before I'll have a real collection, and unfortunately most of the kinds I lack are choice and expensive. So I am taking my time and am turning somewhat to collecting American furniture to go with my weights."

The way this Iowa woman started is typical of many other collectors. A chance circumstance makes some pleasing antique available, and the collecting germ develops. About that time the novice ought to read something about the antiques he has started to collect. Most public libraries have books on the subject, and probably some magazines. He can begin by reading these, and later add those he has found most helpful to his own library. With this added knowledge he will know better what type of antiques he wants to collect. If, as sometimes happened in what collectors call the good old days, he has family connections living in long-established homes, attics or storerooms may yield an antique or two. If that should happen the beginner would be in luck, but it occurs less frequently these days. Neglected, well-filled attics are fewer, and most of them have been already combed by other enthusiasts.

So for most people who want antiques for their homes, either starting from scratch or putting them with a few inherited pieces, the best way is to go out and buy them. If one lives in one of the older parts of the country, it is possible to find people who have some little regarded furniture or other antiques they will sell, but locating such places cannot be done off-hand. More often one comes home empty-handed from such a quest, or with something of questionable age or merit, purchased "just to buy *something* after all the trouble I've made."

It is much easier and usually more productive to go antiquing in the most logical places—the antique shops. Start with the one nearest home and gradually widen your circle. They may seem frightening at first, especially to one who has but recently been started on the road to collecting by the chance acquirement, by gift or inheritance, of a few things, such as a table, a chair, a chest of drawers, a candlestick or an assortment of old dishes. So many things are on display, most of them obviously superior, even to the eye of a novice, to what he possesses. Some beginners have told me that when they began collecting they hesitated to go into the antique shops lest they appear ignorant, or lest everything there should prove to be "so terribly expensive." Instead, they would slip into second-hand stores, where they found many things that even they knew were not antiques. Usually they ended by making a purchase that they later discarded. That is the wrong start for a beginner.

The proprietor of a second-hand store deals in things that are just what the name connotes. If there is an antique in the place it is there by accident. Moreover, such a dealer knows little or nothing about antiques, and cares less. He is interested only in selling what he has, and at times is not above suggesting that something *might* be a very good antique. So, at the start keep out of second-hand stores. Later, when some knowledge has been gained and one has plenty of time to shop around, an occasional good antique may be found in such a store at a fairly low price. But until then, it is best to go to one of the antique shops, preferably one of the smaller ones, since they are less bewildering. They can be found almost anywhere, on side streets in cities and large villages and along main-traveled highways.

Pick well-established dealers who have been in the same locality for a number of years. They are jealous of their reputations for fair practice, and stand back of what they say as to age and originality. As much cannot be said for that very small number of dealers who are constantly moving from one location to another and who largely offer "bargains." When such a dealer thinks he has sold about as many of his low-grade antiques as he can in one spot he moves on to a new location.

When I find myself in a strange town I frequently consult the classified section of the local telephone book for a list of dealers' names. Then I visit the shops for which the descriptions seem most promising. In the same way a beginner can learn about a few near-by shops. Antique dealers are friendly people and, while they are primarily in business to make a living, they will take a surprising amount of trouble to help new collectors who honestly want to learn something about antiques. Therefore don't be afraid to ask questions about pieces new to you, or to ask prices. It is a simple way to get some inkling of values. An occasional purchase from the dealers whose shops you visit in your early enthusiasm for antiques will also help to create good feeling.

When I was first collecting I came to know a combination furniture repairman and dealer. His shop was on Columbia Heights, Brooklyn, just around the corner from the first subway stop from New York. This shop was a magnet for me. At least once a week I stopped there on the way home from my office, not always with the intention of buying, but rather to see his newest purchases. Over the years I bought a number of excellent things from Charlie. I still have some of them, including a fifteen-inch pewter plate marked "LQNDON" on which our plum pudding is always served. That buy was clearly a case of beginner's luck, for at that time I knew practically nothing about pewter.

The novice will soon realize, too, that collectors are not the only buyers at such little shops. There are the people, mostly men, who cruise from shop to shop and make a living by buying from one shop and selling to another. Within the trade they are known as "pickers." They make a business, and a surprisingly lucrative one at times, by their ability to spot "sleepers"—i.e., good antiques priced low because their merits have not been recognized—which they peddle to other dealers, generally those with larger shops. Although these pickers sell mostly to dealers, the majority of them are not disinclined to do business with collectors, in a curbstone manner, if they can manage it without offending the dealer in whose shop collector and picker have their chance meeting.

It is surprising how much territory some of these pickers cover in a week. One, very well-known among dealers, is actually a wholesaler. He lives less than two hours away from New York City, and back of his home is a two-story warehouse usually crowded with about every kind of American antique of the better quality. Glass he does not handle, "because it breaks too easily." He is home Saturdays and Sundays. Those are the days when New York City dealers and larger ones in the general vicinity visit him. When they come it is not for individual antiques, but rather for a station wagon load. Furniture is his speciality, and it is surprising how many fine pieces have passed through his hands. Some of the pieces he once owned are now in museum collections. I doubt if the average collector could get into his storehouse; but should he hear that a collector has an antique for sale he would call on him promptly. But he would not sell to a collector: he is a dealer's dealer.

As to the prices dealers pay for the antiques they handle, there seems to be an impression among uninformed people that they are consistently trying to get their merchandise for nothing, or as close to that as possible. Actually, the laws of economics operate with antiques as with other commodities. What is scarce and in demand, be it beefsteak or block-front furniture, is high in price. When the dealer goes out to buy in your home or mine, if he expects to remain in business he cannot offer more for any antique he has a chance to buy than half the price at which he believes he can sell it. Out of this 100 per cent "mark-up" must come the losses he has to absorb for his "stickers" (the good antiques he buys but cannot sell for a profit), as well as the losses he must absorb on antiques that are damaged or broken in handling. This is particularly true with china and glass, since they are especially fragile. The owner of an antique who thinks he could sell it so much more profitably if he only knew the collectors who wanted it is deceiving himself. As a group, collectors are as keen for a bargain as any dealer, and act accordingly.

Another place for the novice to buy is at the numerous antiques shows that are held in almost every section of the country and have become an important factor for both collectors and dealers. Many of them are either yearly or semi-annual events and are well advertised before they open. As a place where a wide variety of antiques can be seen at one time, I know of nothing that can equal a good show. Most of them are managed by people who specialize in promoting such ventures. They vary all the way from small shows of twelve to twenty exhibitors to large ones of a hundred or more booths, in cities like New York, Boston, Philadelphia and Chicago.

The show managers know the antiques trade well and are assiduous in securing as exhibitors dealers with reputations for handling good antiques. They are just as painstaking in discouraging others who are suspected of offering questionable pieces. Some dealers become regular troupers and go from one antiques show to another, remaining away from home for months at a time. Others choose a certain few shows at which they exhibit regularly, and ignore the rest. Most of the show promotors know that they have dual obligations that they must fulfill if their shows are to be successful and become well established. The collector must find enough interesting antiques on display to be worth the price of admission. The dealers must have enough buyers to "make expenses" and go home with a profit. The show that delights dealers is one at which profits on first-day sales cover booth rental, traveling expenses and room and meals for the show's duration. When this happens, word spreads rapidly throughout the trade and the promotor has little difficulty in signing up space for his next show.

Getting collectors to attend a show is one of the promotor's big problems. Besides advertising it locally and in magazines read by collectors, the most aggressive promotors maintain sizable lists of collectors to whom they mail reduced-rate tickets. They also provide exhibitors with blocks of such tickets, which they are urged to mail to their customers. Much of a promotor's profit comes from gate receipts. Booth rentals about cover such expenses as rental of the hall, erecting the booths, travel in obtaining exhibitors and advertising.

Opening day of any well-planned show, and especially of one that has been held for several years, is a special event. All the veteran collectors who can possibly do so make it a point to be there at opening time. They want to have a first look at everything and are always hopeful of finding a real sleeper. I have seen as many as three hundred of these collectors lined up and waiting for the big New York show at the 71st Regiment Armory to open. Such a show also attracts many of the more important dealers. They, too, are there to buy.

Besides this, from the moment the exhibitors arrive and start unpacking, there is lively trading between them right in the midst of all the hubbub of moving in and dressing their booths. A successful dealer once told me that he planned his exhibit at the New York show well in advance so that he could dress his booth quickly, after which, until the public was admitted, he was free to buy from other dealers. He found that the profits he made on what he bought in this way sometimes equaled the cost of his booth.

Because of the advantages of this before-opening business, every effort is made to keep all but actual exhibitors out. However, some non-exhibiting dealers, and even collectors, do manage to crash the gate. This usually brings loud protests to the promotor, who is anything but idle at such a time. Another of his headaches is the problem of the picker who smuggles in small antiques and peddles them from booth to booth. When caught, such a one is made to leave immediately, though that doesn't prevent his coming back. In fact, I once saw a persistent picker thrown out of a show three times in one day.

If one likes antiques, any show, big or little, is usually worth while. It is a good way for the beginner to extend his knowledge, meet dealers he might not otherwise know and nearly always find a few things worth buying. I have been going to these shows for almost twenty years and remember scarcely one at which I did not see antiques I would like to own. A good number of the pieces in my collection I acquired at shows. The large city shows have a particular attraction for collectors, and some travel long distances to attend them. One couple living in the Middle West would delay their annual vacation each year until the time of the fall show in New York. Others I have met there and at other shows come from still farther away.

Finally, there are the auction sales. They are of two kinds: those of important collections, held at nationally known galleries, especially New York and Philadelphia; and the country auctions. For the large city sales, the auction galleries issue elaborate illustrated catalogues in which each lot is described in a paragraph of from fifty to fifteen hundred words, according to its importance. For country sales, the auctioneers usually issue handbills that indicate some of the highlights of the coming sale. At all auctions, a "lot" refers to a piece or group of pieces sold as a unit, to which a serial number has been given.

Country sales are usually held on the premises of the seller, though sometimes, notably in Pennsylvania and Ohio, a hall is rented for the occasion. In the case of important sales at the large galleries, the antiques to be sold are exhibited several days in advance. Going to one of these exhibitions is another excellent way to learn about antiques. Allow several hours. Buy a copy of the catalogue (a dollar is the usual price), and then make the rounds of the entire display, comparing pieces and catalogue descriptions. The latter have been carefully written and are explicit. Of course, they stress the best features of each piece, but they also state type, provenance and age clearly. Take time enough to study those pieces that are of particular interest. Unlike antiques in museums, those in the auction galleries can, within reason, be handled in the course of examination.

If possible, attend the auction sessions and write down the prices in your catalogue. Later reread the catalogue. An assortment of auction catalogues can frequently be of help in identifying different pieces and fixing their dates. In such catalogues, where a lot is a copy, a phrase such as "Chippendale style" will be used instead of one that gives the age and provenance. This is a tacit indication that the gallery does not rate the lot as antique.

Prices realized at the big auctions are, in general, indicative of the worth of the antiques sold, but it should be borne in mind that a number of things govern these prices. Condition of the individual piece is most important. For instance, a fine piece of furniture in untouched condition, with original brasses and no parts restored or replaced, will always bring a much higher price than if it has been refinished and has replacement brasses or some part repaired or replaced.

In ceramics, age cracks, stains or a poor impression of decorative design reduce the price. Mint condition in silver and pewter, together with a complete and clear maker's mark, makes for top prices; while repairs or reconstruction on pieces by even the rarest makers materially reduce values. In the case of glass, chips, cracks, repairs and that cloudiness known as "sick glass" are definite price reducers.

Moreover, if the weather is bad and the buyers at the sale are fewer than usual, prices are apt to be down. On the other hand, if the collection being sold was formed by a well-known collector, it will probably draw a large audience and the prices will range from very good to record high. Sometimes leading museums want certain pieces from such a collection and bid for them. That always runs the price up materially. Besides this, there are always a number of dealers present. Some may be bidding for customers; others are there to get special pieces of unusual merit; and still more are looking for bargains. If the bids are low enough, so that such dealers feel they can buy and resell profitably, they bid systematically and drop out only when the prices go too high for them "to buy for stock." Auctioneers refer to this as the "back of the room dealer cushion."

Smaller city auctions are not as carefully stage-managed. If there are catalogues, they are hardly more than identifying listings of pieces that form the various lots, and should not be considered as guides to age genuineness or provenance. Many fine antiques have been sold at such auctions, but the people who bought them were usually well-informed collectors or experienced dealers. They could act on their own judgment, and paid little attention to the remarks or descriptions of the auctioneer. Veteran dealers frequently have arrangements by which they are notified if any superior antiques are to be sold at such auctions, and are on hand to bid for them.

The country auction is totally different, and is much more informal. Such sales, most often held at houses where the contents are to be sold, begin about ten in the morning and last until late in the afternoon, and are usually completed in one day. An occasional auction may be of two or three days' duration. Not everything sold qualifies as antique, but frequently some excellent antique furniture and the like are among the lots. During the past two or three years prices at some of these country sales have been close to what city dealers would ask for the same kind of antiques. This is because a large number of people, not local residents, have begun going to country auctions. They find them great fun and tend to run the prices up beyond reason. And there are always the dealers.

Often they form a bidding combination, known as a "knock-out," among themselves for the purpose of discouraging individual bids. Dealers in one of these buying slugs are not at all subtle and can often be seen signaling to one another while bidding is in progress. The auctioneers naturally do not like such combinations, and try hard to stop them. After the sale is over, the dealers in a "knock-out" get together and at what amounts to a second auction allocate among themselves the antiques bought. Because of this condition, the beginner should go over the antiques before the sale starts, decide how much he is willing to bid for the things he wants and then stick to those figures. It is well to remember that there will be other sales. Do not be carried away by the excitement and overbid.

An ever-present opportunity to see and learn about antiques that has served many novices well is to be found in museum collections. There are, of course, the large art museums where, in addition to galleries of paintings and sculpture and other works of art, there are separate ones devoted to antiques. There are smaller museums and collections of local historical societies, as well as the more recent group restorations like Williamsburg, Virginia. By frequent visits to the museum nearest him a beginner can soon acquire a basic grasp of American antiques. Before long he will be able to recognize pieces belonging to the various style periods,

such as a Queen Anne highboy or a Chippendale gaming
table, without first having to stop and read the label. But the
labels should not be ignored. Each is a comprehensive de-
scription and ought to be read carefully.

Among the large museums that have especially fine
antiques displayed in period room settings are the Metropolitan Museum of Art, with its American Wing, largest and
most extensive of them all; the Museum of Fine Arts in
Boston, with its celebrated Karolik Collection; the museum
of the Rhode Island School of Design, with its fine display
of block-front furniture by the Goddard-Townsend group of
cabinetmakers of Newport; the Hartford (Conn.) Atheneum,
known for its outstanding collection of furniture of the
Pilgrim century; the Gallery of Fine Art, Yale University,
which, in addition to two or three eighteenth-century interiors of Connecticut houses, has an unusually fine collection
of American silver; the Philadelphia Museum of Art, with
its Pennsylvania Dutch painted furniture and decorative
accessories; and the Art Institute of Chicago, which has
about the finest collection in the United States of Wedgwood
and other eighteenth-century English ceramics. There are
also the Valentine Museum, Richmond, Virginia; the Cincinnati Art Museum; the William Rockhill Nelson Museum,
Kansas City, Missouri; the Detroit Museum of Fine Arts; and
the Henry Ford Collections that are part of the Edison Institute in near-by Dearborn.

In New York City there are three other museums that
should not be missed. They are the Museum of the City of
New York, where silver is a feature; the New York Historical
Society; and the Brooklyn Museum. The latter has several
interiors from old local houses, done in the Holland Dutch
manner, complete with furnishings, as well as comprehensive
displays of American glass, china and pewter.

Small museums and historic houses maintained as
museums, now numbering over two hundred, are located in

various parts of the country. Because they are less extensive and more intimate, they are frequently more fun, and are certainly less exhausting to visit. Their collections have developed from a confusing jumble of "relics" poorly labeled to well-organized groupings dramatically displayed. Some of them have specialized groups of locally made antiques that cannot be equaled elsewhere, such as the museum at Bennington, Vermont, with its collection of Bennington pottery, and the much larger Essex Institute at Salem, Massachusetts, with its outstanding collection of furniture made by Salem cabinetmakers.

There are also a number of private museums that are open to the public, or that collectors can visit by writing for permission. A museum of this type is usually the outward and visible sign of an ardent wealthy collector who has established it as a means of rationalizing his incurable urge to buy more and more antiques. One of the finest is the Wells Museum at Southboro, Massachusetts, which has a remarkable collection of early tools and implements. Also, H. F. duPont has assembled a superb collection of choice American furniture and decorative accessories at his home at Winterthur, Delaware, which is open for several weeks each spring and fall to those who write for tickets in advance. Mr. duPont's collection rivals that of any museum. A visit to it is well worth the effort and time it takes.

Although museum collections should be seen not once but several times, for downright enjoyment probably nothing exceeds an evening with antiques in the home of a collector and friend. Your host is not only ready but bubbling over to tell you all about each piece. You can talk back and handle each item with a freedom impossible elsewhere. In fact, your host will be complimented if a piece of his furniture so impresses you that you get down on your hands and knees to study the decorative details of its feet. Hallmarks on silver and pewter can be studied and the rich coloring of early blown glass admired.

Just one suggestion: no matter how delightful the experience meeting may be, or how much more there is to see or talk about, when the clock strikes midnight, make your farewell and leave. The old adage about short visits holds true even when two antique hounds meet.

CHAPTER III

How to Judge Antique Furniture

A piece or two of old furniture, acquired by either inheritance or purchase, is frequently the beginning of antique collecting. Even for those who have entered the field by another way, such as glass, silver, china or prints, furniture forms a setting for these accessories that were once part of the early American home.

Individual taste is, of course, the prime factor in choosing the type of antique one collects, but in order that the reader may have a sort of yardstick for determining the merits or defects of a particular piece, we shall endeavor in this and following chapters to give him some concrete and practical points on judging the antiques in each of these categories. These should help him to decide whether a chair, table or case piece is in original condition; whether it has been restored and reconditioned within proper limits, or has been so extensively reworked as to be of little value as an antique; and finally, whether it is a deliberate fake or just a copy of an old piece, with no claim to being an antique. If the latter, too often after it has passed through two or three hands the fact that it was originally just an honest copy is not mentioned, or may even be unknown to its present owner.

Furniture, I believe, is easier to judge than other antiques. This is because each piece over the years has acquired certain signs of age and use which cannot be successfully faked. There is, for instance, the mellow tone of wood known as patina. One of my early mentors in detecting the genuine in furniture once told me that to him patina was just another name for complexion. The quality of it on old furniture depends on the care a particular piece has had over the years. Moreover, there are no cosmetics for new wood that can in any way simulate that soft glow that is one of the distinctive features of furniture made over a century or more ago.

In considering a piece of furniture, take time enough to get a general impression of it as a whole. Is its design pleasing? Are its lines graceful and its proportions good? American antique furniture with these attributes is not yet so scarce. So why bother with a piece that lacks them, such as a late Empire table with heavy and cumbersome base? Plenty of excellent old San Domingo mahogany was wasted on it, but it is far from being a good example of what our cabinetmakers could produce. Assuming, then, that the piece passes the test of good design, do the lines of the parts jibe? For instance, are the feet of a slant-top desk of the Chippendale period right for the rest of the piece, or are they of a type you have never seen supporting a similar desk? If the latter, these "wrong" feet can, of course, be removed and replaced by others of correct lines; or you can wait until you find a desk where body and feet started out together.

Look at the finish of the piece. Has it that much desired original varnish, more or less unscratched and unstained, or is the grain and texture of the wood buried under layers of varnish, stain or even paint? Many pieces of American antique furniture are found in such deplorable condition that the dealer must have them repaired and refinished before showing them. As a rule, this reconditioning is well done, and a dealer of reputation will state just how much restoration has taken place. For such a piece the price is naturally less than that asked for one of the same type in original and prime condition.

In genuine antique furniture, marks of the tools used by the old craftsmen can easily be seen on all but the finished surfaces. These were carefully smoothed by fine planes and sandpapered before varnishing, but backboards and other concealed parts were left in such rough condition that the slight ridges and hollows made by the wide-bladed jack plane can be seen or felt. Sometimes, too, the tooth marks of the old up-and-down pit saw, used to cut boards from the log, can be seen. They are always parallel scratches, slightly slanted but never curved in a wide arc. Tooth marks describing a wide arc prove the use of a buzz or circular saw, used in furniture making after the middle of the nineteenth century. Furniture with parts bearing this mark was either made too late to rank as an antique or has been rebuilt. It could also be a fake.

A dovetail joint, as the name implies, is a corner joint of interlocking tenons cut so that the ends are almost twice as wide as the bases. Such joints are rather crude in very early pieces, individual dovetails being sometimes two inches wide. In most American furniture of the eighteenth and early nineteenth centuries, dovetails are about an inch wide and are uniform. In some early factory-made furniture there are dovetail joints with rounded ends. Dovetail joints can best be seen at the corners of drawers and in case pieces where sides, tops and bottoms are fitted together.

Dovetails were also used in other pieces of furniture at points where a strong and tight joint was needed for a leg, apron or other part. In some pieces, especially tables and chairs, pinned mortise and tenon joints were widely used. Here, for certain parts, such as the legs, narrow slots were cut and into them were fitted the projecting tenons of the parts joined to them. Then to make them secure, quarter-inch holes were bored through the joints and wooden pins driven into the holes. In a genuine piece, close scrutiny will disclose that these pins are many-sided instead of round. A perfectly round pin indicates the use of a machine-made dowel, which postdates antique furniture. The presence of such a dowel therefore means that the piece was either made comparatively recently or is an antique that has been taken apart for regluing or reconstruction, and that the man who did the work was too indifferent to replace the many-sided pins. It could also indicate a modern copy of an old piece.

Another thing to observe in furniture is replacement of feet and spliced legs. Sometimes the bracket or the claw-and-ball feet of chests of drawers or other case pieces have been removed or shortened. In refinishing such a piece, the missing feet are either replaced with new ones of appropriate design or, if cut down, built up to proper height. In American Empire pieces, simple turned feet are sometimes replaced by the more decorative carved paw feet. This is not hard to detect, as the carving of the new feet will be sharper than would be the case if they were the same age as the rest of the piece.

In very early examples, the small turned button or knob feet of butterfly and tavern tables may have disappeared or become so worn that replacements are the only answer. This is, of course, justifiable; but since such tables with original feet, though very rare, are more desirable, careful inspection is in order. Replacements are generally too smooth and perfect when compared with the rest of the table. Also a fine cut or groove between the base of the leg and top of the new foot can be seen, or found with the blade of a pocket-knife. Where all is original there is no cut or groove, for leg and foot were turned from a single length of wood.

In the case of cut-off table legs, restoring the piece to its proper height of twenty-seven to twenty-nine inches is accomplished by splicing. Practically anyone with keen eyes and a good pocket glass can detect the diagonal lines of such repair. When the top or the drop leaves of a table are either missing or beyond repair, it is usual to replace them with similar parts taken from another table of the same wood but with an inferior base. Frequently these replacements have to be reduced in size, and here sharp edges and corners or newly made rule joints of bed and leaves are clear indications that such alterations have taken place.

Drawers in a piece of furniture should be taken out and looked over carefully. Here can be seen certain indications of age, origin and genuineness not as readily visible elsewhere. Except where a different wood, such as fancy-grained maple or satinwood, was used for decorative contrast, drawer fronts should be of the same wood as the rest of the piece and should match in grain and tone. Sides, back and bottom of drawers in American pieces were universally made of such soft woods as pine, spruce, yellow poplar or whitewood, as the old cabinetmakers called basswood. Oak is a clear indication that the piece is of English or Continental provenance. In chests of drawers of such origin, there are usually "dust boards" that completely separate each drawer space from that below or above it. American chests of drawers practically never have this refinement.

In the many pieces of American furniture that I have inspected, I found the same kind of soft wood used for all drawer parts of an individual piece. Also, drawer interiors were never shellacked or varnished. The sides were put together with dovetails and the underside of the bottom bore the ridges and hollows left by a jack plane. Sometimes in the small drawers in desk and secretary interiors wooden pins were used in place of dovetailing. A drawer bottom of plywood is a modern replacement. In many old pieces, the lower edges of the drawer sides will have been worn away as much as a half-inch. Frequently this has been repaired with new wood, and the runners on which the drawers slide replaced. Such restoration does not harm a piece, since it is a practical correction that compensates for normal wear.

Labels

From about 1760 to 1830, some of the American cabinetmakers labeled their furniture. The upper side of drawer bottoms, near the front, was a favorite location. The labels were usually printed from type, although a few were handsomely done copper-plate engravings. Some were so simple that they merely gave the maker's name and the town where he worked; others, like the engraved label of Benjamin Randolph, depicted a number of pieces of furniture. This label reads:

> "Benj. Randolph Cabinet Maker at the Golden Eagle
> between third and fourth Streets Philadelphia
> Makes all Sorts of Cabinet & Chair work
> Likewise Carving Gilding etc.
> Performed in the Chinese and Modern Taste."

Randolph was one of the ablest of Philadelphia cabinet-makers who worked in the Chippendale style. It was at his house that Thomas Jefferson lodged in 1776 while attending the Continental Congress. Possibly Randolph may have made the revolving Windsor chair with broad writing arm on which Jefferson wrote the first draft of the Declaration of Independence. It is now owned by the American Philosophical Society and is on display in the Society's library adjoining Independence Hall.

In desks, the labels were sometimes pasted on the back of the small door in the center of the interior, between the pigeonholes; in sideboards, on the back of one of the cupboard doors; and in tall case clocks, on the back of the long narrow door of the lower section.

A label adds materially to the value of a piece and should be protected. A good way to do this is to cover it with a piece of cellophane held in place by strips of adhesive tape. An unusual label that I saw recently was hand-lettered in ink on part of a page torn from an account book.

Forged labels have proved too much of a temptation to some unscrupulous dealers. A favorite practice is to clip the advertisement of a cabinetmaker from an old newspaper or city directory, or even to use the letterhead of an old bill, and paste it to a piece of old furniture as a label. This type of faking can be recognized by the lack of decorative borders and the difference in typography. In those made from newspaper advertisements, the smallness of type is noticeable. Moreover, if such a "label" is moistened and removed, the printing on the back will serve as a give-away. Genuine labels never had any printing on the reverse side.

In some pieces, like the fine American Chippendale desk in the American Wing at the Metropolitan Museum, the name of the maker may be found done in pencil on the underside of a drawer. In this desk the inscription reads: "This desk was made in the year 1769 by Benj. Burnam who served his time in Filadelphia." This eighteenth-century cabinetmaker was born in Connecticut and worked in Hartford, but went to Philadelphia for his apprenticeship.

In the case of Windsor chairs especially, a name was sometimes branded on the underside of the seat with a hot iron. It might be that of the maker or of the original owner. That the latter's name was occasionally so used is shown by a Windsor branded "John Jay." This chair was one of a set which the first Chief Justice of the United States Supreme Court had made, possibly by a New York craftsman. It was acquired by its present owner from a Jay descendant.

Occasionally the maker's name was stamped on a piece of furniture with a steel die in quarter- to half-inch capital letters. This was a standard practice with French ebenists. When found on American furniture it indicates that its maker was probably one of the French workers who migrated to the United States during the unsettled times that commenced with the Reign of Terror and continued through the Napoleonic period.

A gaming table, once attributed to Duncan Phyfe, in the Benkard Room at the Museum of The City of New York, is so marked with the name "Lannuier" on the edge of a drawer side. Lannuier worked in New York from 1790 to

1819, probably at first as a journeyman of Phyfe, but by 1805
he had established his own shop. Other pieces from his hands
have either a simple printed label or an elaborate one with
wording in both French and English.

His contemporary, Duncan Phyfe, evidently did not put
labels on his furniture except in rare instances, and then only
when it was to be shipped far from New York. Less than a
dozen labeled Phyfe pieces are known so far, most of them
found in the South. The Brooklyn Museum has a pair of
rosewood window benches decorated with gilt stenciling, on
one of which is his autograph. This signature, "D.Phyfe," is
done in ink on the coarse white textile stretched over the
springs beneath the removable cushion. These benches were
originally owned by a customer living in Fayetteville, North
Carolina. Two different printed labels of this self-effacing
cabinetmaker are known. The earlier one bears the address,
35 Partition Street; and the later one, *170 Fulton Street.*
One such label, dated August, 1820, reads: "D.Phyfe's
CABINET WAREHOUSE, No. 170 Fulton street, New
York. N. B. Curled Hair Matrasses, Chair and Sofa Cushions."

Grandfather clocks are apt to have the maker's name on
the dial, and the label of the cabinetmaker who produced the
case attached to the back of the long door. Labels are also
found on the back of many mirror frames. John Elliot, who
worked in Philadelphia from 1753 to about 1780, used a
label that was printed in both English and German. Charles
DelVecchio, a New York maker of mirror glass and frames
from about 1801 to 1830, at times used a label printed in
Spanish, evidently for his West Indian trade. The last line
of this label stated: "C.Del Vecchio speaks Spanish, French,
English and Italian."

Chairs

Many chairs are found with shortened legs. Much of
this mutilation was due to the rocking-chair mania which

swept America between 1780 and 1830. Householders, either too thrifty or too impoverished to buy one of the new-fangled things outright, often improvised by taking a straight chair and cutting off from two to five inches of the legs, depending on the width and curve of the rockers that were added. So chairs with seats less than sixteen or eighteen inches from the floor were probably altered into rockers or were cut down for slipper chairs, as low-seated chairs used in bedrooms were called.

In the days when women wore multiple petticoats and skirts that swept the floor, putting on high button shoes was an undertaking that could be made a little easier if one sat in an armless low chair. Hence, some odd chair or one from a bedroom set was used to provide this aid in dressing, from two to four inches being cut off the legs. Since slipper chairs did not receive hard or frequent use, many of them have survived to plague present-day collectors.

Sometimes, too, one finds both arm and side chairs with about an inch of the legs missing and castors added. This, I believe, provided a chair for a semi-invalid in which he could propel himself about his room. I have a slat-back armchair of about 1780, all in original condition save for leg amputation. When I acquired it, some years ago, it was mounted on a wide heavy board with four two-inch wheels attached. It had been the favorite chair of an early breeder of Merino sheep who had become so crippled that he walked with utmost difficulty. Being an ingenious Vermonter, he had this chair converted into a primitive version of the modern wheel chair. Since the seat is almost sixteen inches high, I have never had it restored, even though the lower rungs almost rest on the floor.

In the case of a chair where the seat is so low as to be uncomfortable, there is only one way to regain the proper height. This is to splice the shortened legs. It is a proper repair and frequently done, but one does not like to buy a chair thinking it all original, only to discover later that the legs have been pieced. Where this has been done the lap is not hard to see, and there will be slight difference in the color and grain of the added pieces. With a painted chair, a close look may disclose the fine lines that mark the presence of lapped joints.

Queen Anne fiddle-back chairs with Flemish scroll feet ought to be checked carefully. In some, the feet may be half worn away; in others, one or all may have been replaced with new ones made secure by a long dowel extending up into the leg. When this has been done, the carving of the new feet will be sharp, and free from the minor dents of long usage, and there will probably be a slight difference in tone and grain of wood. Here again the knife-blade test can be used to find the joining of old legs and new feet.

Another repair common in slat-back chairs is replacing the urn- or vase-shaped finials of the back uprights. It can usually be recognized by the pristine freshness of the new finials. Also, the difference in tone and grain between them and the rest of the uprights, as well as the line showing where the new finials were attached, are additional clues.

Occasionally the pad or duck foot on the front leg of a Queen Anne chair or the carved claw-and-ball foot on a Chippendale chair is broken or partly missing. To repair it, the edge is planed smooth and a small block of wood is firmly glued in place and then shaped to conform to the original design. Again, this can be detected by the line of the joint and the difference between the old wood and the added piece.

In the case of arm or side chairs having vase-shaped or pierced back splats, it is well to look for evidence that such splats have not at some time been broken by accident or abuse. Tilting backward in a chair so that the front legs are free of the floor was an almost sure-fire method of breaking the splat or wrenching it from its location and splintering the lower cross member into which it was mortised. It could also break the tenon joints by which the sides of the seat frame were joined to the back legs. Repairs of such breaks can be seen by the lines where broken pieces were glued together.

All of these repairs, from splicing shortened legs to replacing an entire leg or a missing cross stretcher, are legitimate; but a chair on which such work has been done is, naturally, not as valuable as one all in original condition. Therefore the price should be correspondingly less. If the collector believes a chair under consideration may have been so repaired, he should not hesitate to ask the dealer. If it has occurred, the dealer will be willing to go over the piece and point out just what work has been done on it.

Before the days of modern plumbing, a commode chair was not an uncommon piece of bedroom furniture and a Windsor armchair was frequently adapted to such a use. With old pieces so mutilated, the only practical repair is to fit in a circular block of wood of the same thickness as the seat. No matter how skillfully done, the repair is clearly visible, but it is justified, since some of the best examples of old Windsors have had to be so restored.

A casualty with comb-back Windsors is apt to be one or both of the delicate scroll-carved ends of the comb piece. Here repair is achieved by gluing small blocks of wood to the broken ends, which are then shaped and carved to conform to the original design. Again, new carving, difference of grain and tone of wood tell where this necessary restoration has been done.

As for repairs that took place long before Windsors were collected as antiques, I know of a bow-back armchair where the hoop was broken at one of the spindles. The original owner repaired it by binding a two-inch piece of leather around the fracture. Then he balanced it by a similar wrapping on the other curve of the bow. This New Hampshire chair was repaired in this manner more than seventy-five years ago. At that time the wrappings were painted the same dark green as the rest of the piece. A neat and unobtrusive repair, it has held fast down to the present day.

All old Windsor chair seats were shaped from a single piece of wood ranging from an inch and a half to two and a half inches in thickness. Sometimes such seats cracked and were repaired by gluing or inserting dowels. Such repairs could nowise cause them to be confused with the factory-made chair of the 1890's, with its seat formed of two, three or even four pieces of wood glued together before shaping. During the last decade of the nineteenth century there was a revival in the popularity of Windsors. Since then, quantities of bow-back armchairs have been bought for libraries, clubs, Y.M.C.A. rooms and similar public places. Some of these factory-made Windsors with obvious signs of age and much use are occasionally offered as antiques, but they can be distinguished by their pieced seats, plainer turnings of legs and stretchers, heavier back spindles, thicker arms and uncarved hand-pieces, the latter frequently formed by gluing blocks of wood to the arm ends.

American Windors were made of an assortment of native hard woods with soft wood for the seats. Those of England were, except for the seats, all of one wood. Yew was a favorite but elm and beech were also used. Many English Windsors have, in addition to the spindles, a central pierced back splat with a wheel-like motif dominating the design; and there is also less splay to the legs than with American-made examples. Consequently they can be easily distinguished from those made here. They are good antiques, but in my opinion they belong in collections of English provincial furniture.

On Windsors, slat-backs, and corner chairs made of turned parts, if one examines the front legs and back uprights, faint scored lines can be seen. These were made with the blade of a chisel, at the time the parts were turned, as guides for the places where holes were to be bored for cross stretchers, or where mortises were to be cut for the back slats.

Such scored lines are clear indications of age and genuineness.

Early furniture factories and craft workshops in the Southern mountains produced slat-back chairs. Some of them may have been around for better than seventy years, but they are not antiques. They can usually be recognized either by lack of finials on the back uprights, or, if present, by their simple steeple shape. Stretchers and slats are heavier, and the entire chair is of one wood. In antique chairs, front and back uprights were usually of maple or yellow birch; oak, hickory or ash were among the woods used for slats and sometimes for stretchers.

In the days of one- and two-power candlelight, the slat-back was much favored in many households as a reading chair, especially in the evening when it was a common practice to hang a pair of wrought-iron tubular candlesticks of the "hog-scraper" type on the back of the top slat near the uprights. As a result, the upright finials and even the slat were often charred by the candle flames. Such charred spots are signs of use that bespeak genuineness.

In the case of sofas and upholstered chairs, particularly the wing type, made in the Queen Anne and Chippendale periods, about the only way to judge for originality is by the look of legs and other parts of the visible framework, unless it has been stripped of upholstery and the condition of the soft wood frame can be studied. When such a piece is in the rough, the presence of coarse old hand-woven linen as covering for the stuffing of seat and back is a good indication of age. Because of the difficulty in judging the merits of either a sofa or upholstered armchair, the collector would be wise to depend on a well-informed and experienced dealer of good reputation. His bill of sale for such a piece will state explicitly approximate age, provenance and any unusual restorations that have been necessary in reconditioning it. The price may be somewhat higher than that of one bought "as is," but in my opinion it is worth the difference.

One important dealer whom I know takes a series of photographs of each wing chair he handles. He starts with it as it comes to him, shows steps in the removal of the upholstery, until it is down to the frame, which is photographed twice, as is and again as repaired and strengthened before being re-upholstered. Such care is justified, because a good, original wing chair is never inexpensive.

The tripod table was a popular piece of American furniture from the Chippendale period through that of the American Empire. It varied in design from a large one with circular top and handsome cabriole legs to a light stand size with a round, oval or lozenge-shaped top. There are distinct points to be observed in considering such a table, be it large, medium or small. Is it all of the same wood? Contrasting woods were seldom used. Are the legs original? Is the three-pronged wrought-iron plate that strengthened the joining of legs and upright shaft still in place? If the top tilts, it should have the original brass latch in an elaborate table, or a wooden button in a simpler example.

If the top is circular, measure the diameter with the grain of the wood and again across the grain. If original, there will be a variance of from three-eights to three-quarters of an inch. This is because wood shrinks slightly across the grain, as it ages but never with the grain. In some elaborate tables in the Chippendale style, the rims of the circular tops are scalloped and have deep carved borders. These are called piecrust tables. To make such a top, the old craftsmen used an extra thick piece of wood to allow for the carving. When that was completed the balance of thickness was cut away to make a flat surface about three-quarters of an inch thick. A piecrust table in original condition is rare and valuable. Consequently one must be on guard against a plain circular top that has been glorified by the addition of a piecrust rim. This is achieved by gluing additional wood on the edge in about thirty-two short pieces lapjointed together, and then carving them to simulate an original piecrust design. In a table top having a raised molding, commonly known as a "dish-top," no new wood is added. Instead, the plain rim is carved and the rest of the table top is planed away to the unusual thinness of about a half-inch. A table that has undergone either of these glorifications no longer rates as a genuine antique, and is therefore not a desirable purchase as such.

During the past twenty-five years many small tilt-top tables have been made that somewhat resemble antique examples. They are usually about twenty inches high, with plywood tops. Made to sell as coffee tables or to go beside an armchair, they should not be mistaken for antiques. Old tilt-tops were never less than twenty-six inches high, and their tops were of solid wood rather than plywood, which is a modern material.

The butterfly table takes its name from the two winglike swinging brackets that support the leaves of the top. Such tables are of southern New England origin and date from about 1680 to 1730. It is now thought that most of them were made in the various villages of Connecticut. They were usually of maple, though cherry was also used. Occasionally one is found in which several native woods make up the base, and the top is of maple, cherry or even pine. As most butterfly tables were finished with the red paint known as New England red filler, this difference in woods did not matter. Wherever possible, this original finish should be preserved in preference to refinishing in natural wood color.

Most butterfly table tops, with the drop leaves raised, are oval, oblong, or square. Rarely are they round. They measure about 36 inches long by 40 to 44 inches wide, and the height of a genuine old example, with turned feet intact, is between 25 and 27 inches.

Butterfly tables are among the high-priced rarities. An all original one in good condition runs into a tidy sum of money. Over a period of more than two hundred years, the small turned feet are apt to have become worn down or to have disappeared. New feet are the answer, and can be detected in the usual ways. The top also may be from a later table, cut down to fit the base. The long narrow drawer, located in the bed of the base, should have a turned wooden knob and sometimes the front will be made of curly maple for contrast.

Because of their rarity and high value, one must be on guard against the unscrupulous or uninformed dealer who offers a changeling rebuilt from one of the large joined stools, made just a little earlier than the butterfly table. These seventeenth-century pieces have the same construction of four turned sloping legs and plain stretchers. To such a stool, wing-shaped supports and a drop-leaf top made of old wood have been added. However, the edges of these parts will be too sharp and perfect, and the difference in the tone of wood will be marked enough for the careful observer to read the story. Still easier to recognize are tables of butterfly design produced fifteen or twenty years ago by Western furniture factories with no intent to deceive. In them, the parts of the base are of smaller dimensions and are not held together with wooden pegs. Also, the tops are apt to be made of narrow strips of wood, glued together.

The gate-leg table, so called because of the resemblance of its two or four swinging legs to a fence gate, was made about the same time as the butterfly, in all the American colonies from Pennsylvania to Maine. These tables, with the parts of their bases turned in ring, vase or bobbin shapes, were never made with the sloping or canted legs of the butterfly table. The material used was the native hard woods. Some were entirely of curly maple, and some, dating as late as 1760, were of mahogany.

The tables varied in size from very small occasional ones to those large enough to serve as a dining table for eight or even ten people. Although not as rare as the butterfly, an all original gate-leg table with well-turned legs and stretchers is by no means cheap. The usual replacement of feet, legs, stretchers and top may be expected, and should be watched for in buying. Many of our furniture factories have made tables of this design for at least twenty years, but differences in wood and construction, as in new butterfly tables, will indicate this. The factory-made pieces have smaller turned parts, and some even have plywood tops.

About 1790, with the introduction of the Hepplewhite style and continuing through the American Empire period, a new kind of dining table came into use. It consisted of a set of two, three or even four tables that could be used with or without the leaves raised, according to the number of people to be seated. These tables were mostly of mahogany, though a few were of maple or cherry. Those in the Hepplewhite style had slender, square tapering legs; the Sheraton ones had turned and reeded legs; in the American Empire slightly heavier turned legs were carved in leaf motifs. In England many such tables in the Regency style had pedestal bases supported by concave branching legs, which were often reeded on top and terminated with brass box-caster ends. These English tables are more plentiful today than American-made examples of the same period.

In buying a two- or three-part table, make sure that all parts started out together, Sometimes, to go with a pair of original ends, an odd drop-leaf table of the same style is cut down to match the pair for size. This can be detected, both by the usual tests as to wood tones and new edges, and by turning the tables over so that the unvarnished part of the frame can be studied. If all three parts are original, the structural elements will be of the same soft woods. Similar tests can be made with a matching pair of double-topped card tables. Through the years such pairs tend to become separated through division of family heirlooms or other circumstances; consequently they are hard to find today.

Likeness of wood and workmanship are the best indications that both tables were made by the same craftsman at the same time.

Sideboards

Contemporary with these console card tables and three-part dining tables was the sideboard, originally developed by Thomas Shearer, London craftsman and furniture designer. Mahogany was the favored wood for this dining-room piece, but cherry and maple were also used. Sometimes mahogany or cherry formed the carcass, and drawers and doors were of light-colored woods, such as fancy-grained maple or satinwood. Many of the American Hepplewhite sideboards were elaborately decorated with inlay medallions and banding.

Since these sideboards were frequently very large—seven to eight feet long and nearly four feet high—when they went out of fashion some seventy years ago many seem to have gravitated to barns and hen houses. There they were used as a storage place for odds and ends of harness or as poultry nests. When recovered, they were naturally in bad condition, with some parts missing. Moreover, because their size is overpowering for many modern homes, some of them have either been completely rebuilt or reduced in size by deleting the end parts with their deep cupboards. It is wise to examine such a piece carefully for new wood, indications of rebuilding or cutting down, replacement of doors and drawers, as well as inlay repaired or added to glorify an original but plainer sideboard. Carefully restored and even made smaller, such a sideboard is a perfectly usable piece of furniture, although its value as an antique is naturally reduced.

For the collector who wants a small sideboard that will fit the available space in his dining room, there are a number of other choices. A few sideboards about five feet long were made by American cabinetmakers in the Hepplewhite and

Sheraton styles. Rare and in demand, they are correspondingly expensive. In New England a good number, made in the Sheraton and American Empire styles, are similar in outline to a good-sized chest of drawers, and these are not over three feet six inches long. They do not have the tall cupboards at either end, but have one in the center beneath a wide shallow drawer; it is flanked by two narrow but deep drawers, originally designed for liquor bottles. These sideboards are handsome and charming pieces. Some are simple examples of country cabinetry; others are more elaborate, having been made by such skilled craftsmen as the group who worked in Salem, Massachusetts, during the first quarter of the nineteenth century.

At the same time that such sideboards were being made in the North, a much simpler piece known as a hunt board was being produced from Maryland southward. It was usually made of southern pine or red walnut, and was somewhat taller than other sideboards. Workmanship was on the crude side, with no effort at ornamentation. These hunt boards are now in great demand for country use.

Lastly, for those who are not insistent that a sideboard be of American provenance, many English-made ones in the Hepplewhite, Sheraton and Regency styles are to be found in our antique shops. They are not over four feet in length, and are generally a little less expensive than those made in America.

Desks and Secretaries

Desks were first made by American cabinetmakers about 1700, and secretaries with upper sections fitted with doors and shelves were made just a few years later. They appeared in all of the styles, from William and Mary through the Early Victorian. Some were made with slanting lids, others with "fall fronts," and still others had a folding writing flap. These desks and secretaries offer the collector a wider variety of types and designs than do almost any other pieces, save possibly chests of drawers, chairs and tables.

Since all but the countinghouse desk, which is essentially a writing box mounted on a leg framework, are case pieces with a series of drawers beneath the writing section, in judging them for condition and originality, one should inspect them as one would a chest of drawers. Look at feet and drawers for indications of possible replacements or reconstructions. With a slant-top desk, be sure the lid is original and not a replacement made of old wood. In the case of pigeonholes and small drawers of the interior, the wood should be thin, not over a quarter to three-eights of an inch thick. The tone of the unvarnished sides, backs and bottoms of these small pine, spruce or whitewood drawers should be a clear light yellow. A good test is to take them out and replace them upside down. The old cabinetmakers were such careful workmen that drawers of their making will slide back and forth just as readily upside down. Replacements, on the other hand, frequently bind when submitted to this test.

As for woods, American desks and secretaries of the William and Mary and Queen Anne periods were of walnut, maple, cherry or sometimes birch. During the Chippendale era the favorite woods were walnut, mahogany and sometimes cherry or maple. The Hepplewhite, Sheraton and American Empire styles favored mahogany, cherry or maple, with drawer fronts sometimes made of fancy-grained maple or satinwood veneer. Some desks were also ornamented with lines of inlay or nicely done medallions, such as a sunburst or an eagle.

In repairing and reconditioning a desk, carving or inlay is sometimes added with the idea of "prettying up" an otherwise simple piece. Such glorification is as easily detected here as in other pieces.

Since the top and bottom of secretaries are separate, it sometimes happens that parts from two different pieces have

UPPER LEFT: Blade from early cabinetmaker's jack plane. RIGHT: How back boards of genuine American pieces should look with ridges and hollows made by jack plane. Such rough smoothing was done by American cabinetmakers as late as 1835. Only surfaces that showed were completely smoothed and sandpapered. LOWER LEFT: Old furniture back boards were frequently very knotty. The inside surface should look like this, planed smooth but never varnished or painted, so the grain of the wood and slight bruises show clearly. RIGHT: Upper side of drawer bottom. Here the grain of the unvarnished but smoothed soft woods and accidental stains can be clearly seen.

ABOVE: HOW THE UNDERSIDE OF A DRAWER BOTTOM SHOULD LOOK
Taken from the small drawer of an antique light stand, this shows characteristic rough planing. At sides and top can be seen chamfered planing done to make the board thin enough to fit into the quarter-inch grooves of the drawer front and sides.

BELOW: OLD AND NEW SAW MARKS COMPARED
At right is a piece of wood sawed by straight saw used by old American cabinetmakers to cut boards from the log. Notice the straight parallel scratches left by the teeth of coarse ripping saw. Left, curved marks of modern buzz saw. When such marks are found on a piece of furniture they are clear indications of new work. The old cabinetmakers did not have these power-driven circular saws.

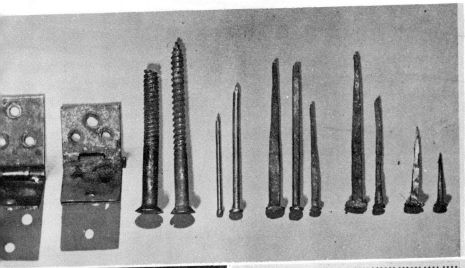

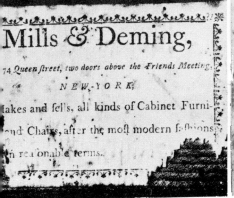

OLD AND NEW NAILS, SCREWS AND HINGES COMPARED

Right to left: The first four are various sizes of hand-made nails taken from a piece of antique American furniture. They were used to attach back boards and the like. The next three items are out nails used on furniture from about 1830. Two modern machine-made wire nails; a hand-filed and a machine-made screw. The worm of the hand-made example is irregular and its point is blunt. A hand-forged and a machine stamped iron hinge. The leaves of the hand-made one are of two-thicknesses and slightly irregular; the leaves of the other are of one thickness and perfectly regular.

At the left is the label of Mills & Deming of New York as pasted on the back of one of their fine Hepplewhite sideboards. At the right, an advertisement like this is carefully trimmed and attached to a piece of furniture to look like maker's label. The difference in typography and the absence of a border make it easy to detect the fraudulent.

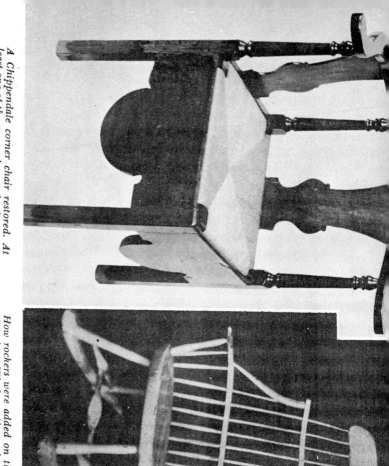

A Chippendale corner chair restored. At least one of the square legs and other parts including one of the back splats have been overly restored or possibly replaced. Otherwise, except for the seat, is original and was refinished with three coats of shellac polished with wax.

How rockers were added on this unusual American Windsor. About three inches of the legs were cut off and the rockers attached with lap joints and screws. The under side of the rockers are flattened from years of use, showing that this conversion was made fully a century ago.

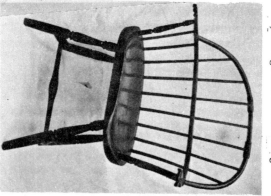

Windsor chair repaired many years ago. Farm-made at Unity, New Hampshire, about 1830, a break in the hoop at one of the spindles was repaired by wrapping it with leather. For balance this was repeated on the other side of the central spindle. This home-done repair took place over 75 years ago and is still strong.

LEFT: American Highboy of 1700. This William and Mary piece is made of basswood and still retains its original painted finish of brown ground color and black graining lines applied freehand. The front is grained in a pattern that simulates walnut oyster grain veneering. The teardrop drawer pulls are contemporary but not original as plugged holes show that at one time bail handles were substituted. Trumpet-form legs, shaped stretchers and bun feet are all original which is unusual in a piece as old as this. The wide torus molding in the cornice conceals a secret drawer. This highboy is believed to have been made in the Hoarkill Valley of northeastern Pennsylvania. Height, 5 feet, 10 inches; width 3 feet, 8 inches; depth, 22 inches. To preserve its original finish, the surface has been hand polished with beeswax and turpentine.

RIGHT: Decorative detail of painted highboy. Side of upper half showing "Tree of Life" motive also primitive figures of bird at left and Quaker at right.

TOP LEFT: Normal wear of drawer sides. The slightly curved under-edges of the drawer and its downward slant come from years if use. This can be remedied by thin strips on the under side and by replacing runners. RIGHT: A New England mirror ca. 1820. In untouched condition, it shows average marks of wear and use. The fruit group in upper panel was painted on back of glass. THE ROCKER (Helen Ormsbee Collection) is in original condition. Both stencil decoration and some of the graining of front roll could be easily restored.

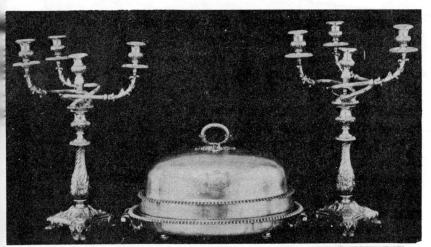

English Silver and Sheffield Plate. The pair of candelabras were made in London and are fully hall marked but these are now clear enough to establish the date letter or the maker's mark. The footed domed serving dish is Sheffield plate made circa 1800.

An American silver tea service. In classic Adam design it was made circa 1790. It bears the touch mark of one of the American silversmiths not identified.

ABOVE LEFT: Early American Glass. A pair of off-hand mold-blown pitchers in deep cobalt blue, probably made at some South Jersey glass house circa 1825, and a blown footed wine glass possibly made by an early New England glass factory before 1840. RIGHT: a satin glass pitcher. Made by some American glass factory about 1885, the background is a pastel shade of blue with frost clear-glass handle. BELOW LEFT: Pair of early pressed glass whale oil lamps. Made about 1840, they retain their gold leaf decoration which is seldom found on such lamps. RIGHT: A typical piece of lacy Sandwich glass. This is a deep vegetable dish 10 by 8½ inches and is a rare piece found only in clear glass.

been assembled, with the larger reduced in width and depth to match the other. Usually traces of new work are a definite clue. If original, both parts should be of the same wood and correspond in grain and color. Where the doors of the upper half are glazed, it is well to make sure that the fine moldings or muntins that separate the small pieces of glass are not new work, installed when the original wooden panels were removed. Similarly, if the secretary has a carved cornice or a broken pediment bonnet top, either of which adds materially to value if original, be sure that such features are not replacements or additions applied to a plain flat-topped piece. Lastly, with black walnut desks or secretaries of the Early Victorian period, look for evidences of handwork. The best of them were so done, and are much more desirable now than later ones produced in factories with practically all of the work done by machinery.

Highboys and Lowboys

Like the secretary, the highboy, made in America from about 1690 to 1775 in the William and Mary, Queen Anne and Chippendale styles, was also a two-part piece. During the first two periods, highboys were made of walnut, maple, both plain and curly, and occasionally cherry. In the designs of Chippendale, walnut or mahogany was usual, though a few country pieces were made of maple or cherry. Some early highboys were made of a soft wood, such as basswood, sweet gum or white pine. These were all painted originally.

When the collection of the late George Horace Lorimer was dispersed at auction, I was lucky enough to acquire a William and Mary highboy made of basswood and painted to simulate walnut, with drawer fronts neatly grained to resemble burl walnut or oyster veneering. Five feet ten inches tall and three feet eight inches wide, it is typical in size of many of the early American highboys. As it has dust boards separating the drawer spaces, it was probably made by a recently arrived European-trained cabinetmaker, since this type of construction is seldom found in native chests of drawers, or kindred pieces. It also has the flat top characteristic of all highboys prior to the middle of the Queen Anne period. It has six delicately turned trumpet legs and shaped stretchers, and its ball feet are not only intact but in surprisingly good condition considering the fact that the piece was made some two hundred and forty years ago.

In the Queen Anne style, four cabriole legs replaced the earlier trumpet-shaped ones. Carving was added to the square central drawer fronts of the upper and lower sections during the latter part of the period and became very elaborate in some of the highboys made in the Chippendale style, especially those of the Philadelphia cabinetmakers. Many of these late Queen Anne and Chippendale pieces have either a broken pediment or an enclosed bonnet top and flame- or urn-shaped finials.

In examining a highboy for indications of genuineness or traces of reconstruction, regard it as you would a chest of drawers. Then consider the legs to be sure they have not been cut off and repaired by splicing, or even replaced by new ones. Occasionally one finds a reproduction highboy, particularly in the Chippendale style, made twenty to fifty years ago that shows signs of age and use. By looking at the interior, differences of workmanship and traces of buzz-saw cutting will identify it as a copy. Also, since tops and bases all too often tend to become separated in the course of time, be certain that the piece under consideration is not a "married" one, assembled from stray bottom and top sections, as indicated with secretaries.

Since the chest-on-chest is still another two-part piece, is should be examined in much the same way as a highboy. If it has a bonnet top, study the moldings and carvings for the possibility of too extensive replacements or added carving.

Lowboys were companion pieces to highboys. Some,

especially during the Chippendale years, were produced to match their taller relatives. As they served more or less as dressing tables they measured from twenty-nine to thirty-one inches in height. Highboy bases are four to six inches higher, and larger in proportion. So if an oversized lowboy is offered, it is apt to be the base of a highboy to which a table top has been added. A Solomon act was frequently performed when two heirs wanted the same highboy in the course of property division. With feet added, the upper part became a chest of drawers; while the lower was converted to a dressing table or lowboy.

A collector I know spotted a transformed upper part some years ago in a Connecticut farmhouse and found the sister of its owner had the base. This division had apparently not resulted in peaceful settlement, since the two women had not been on speaking terms for years. By using diplomacy and patience, the collector finally bought both parts and reunited them, though not the sisters.

Beds

Although handsome beds were made by American cabinetmakers in the Chippendale manner, they are rarities and costly. Most antique beds found in antique shops are in the Hepplewhite, Sheraton and Empire styles. Up to 1820, most four-posters were from six to eight feet tall. Then came the low ones, with posts from four to five feet tall. By modern standards these old beds are too short and too narrow. Consequently some strange conversions are wrought by repairmen to suit customers.

These include converting two beds with similar turnings into a pair of twin beds. Also, in order to get the desired length and width, the original side and end rails are discarded or made longer by splicing. Since the turned posts of many low-post beds are on the heavy side, some reconditioners have them re-turned on a lathe, thus reducing the size an inch or more. All of these changes seem to me unwise, as the results are rebuilt antiques of doubtful value. Personally, I am against buying beds that have been so reworked or having drastic changes made in beds bought in original condition. I am for either using old beds as they are, except for installing brackets on side rails to support the modern spring; or buying modern beds of simple lines. For instance, a box spring mounted on four simply turned mahogany legs is an innocuous piece for use with antique furniture.

The side and end rails of original four-post beds should bear chisel marks done in Roman numerals that correspond to those on the posts. It is a form of labeling, and where the size and style of numbering differ, it is an indication that missing rails have been replaced by those from another bed. In both high- and low-post beds, the wood of rails and posts was usually the same, but the headboards were frequently cut from a wide piece of soft wood, such as pine. In a bed originally lacking these large iron screws used to make posts and rails firm, dealers have them so fitted before refinishing. This is desirable, since with the bolts and with iron brackets to support the spring, an antique bed becomes a perfectly usable piece of modern household furniture.

Painted Chairs

From about 1815 to 1840, a large number of painted fancy chairs were made in American shops that specialized in producing and decorating them. Hitchcock, who worked in a small hamlet near Winsted, Connecticut, was one of these specialists. He made such fine painted fancy chairs that his name is now synonymous with them. Those that retain their original stenciled designs, done in gilt and colors, are the most desirable. Others that have been redecorated are sometimes so well done that at first glance they could be mistaken for originals. Such redecorating is perfectly proper if the chairs are not offered as in original condition. Other Hitchcocks are reconditioned by painting the entire surface black or a very dark green. In such a case the price should be somewhat less than for the redecorated chairs.

Along with the painted fancy chair, but not made quite as early, came the comfortable Boston rocker, which was also decorated by stenciling in gilt and color. Sometimes the design of one of these is worn in spots and is renewed by "touching up," which is a proper restoration; others are completely redecorated, as are the fancy chairs. A Boston rocker in original condition is a desirable antique. Those that have been redecorated are not as good, and even less desirable are others that have been stripped of all paint and refinished with shellac in natural wood color.

Mirrors

Another instance of value reduced is in the too thorough refurbishing of mirror frames. If the frame is one of the Chippendale type that combines mahogany with gilded carving, the latter may have been replaced in part or entirely regilded. In the same way, an old gilded frame that has been given a new coat of gold leaf may gleam like a fresh-washed infant, but its value as an antique would be considerably higher if it were allowed to keep its original complexion, though dulled by age and even chipped in places.

In tabernacle and similar type mirrors, the upper painted glass panel may be cracked or otherwise in bad condition, or it may be missing. A replacement, painted in the old spirit, is a legitimate restoration, but such a mirror is not worth over half or two-thirds as much as one with its original picture intact. As for antique mirror glass, it is not unusual for the silvering to be discolored or even disintegrated in spots. There is no way of correcting this, so the collector must either be content to regard himself in a glass darkly or get a modern mirror.

Nails

In most antique furniture the old cabinetmakers used only nails to hold back boards in place. The presence of them gives an important clue as to the approximate age of a piece. Until about 1810 all nails were hand-forged. Then came the cut nails, which were squarish tapered bits cut by a stamping machine from flat sheets of iron about a quarter of an inch thick. These cut nails have a head not much larger than the upper end of the shank. The other end is blunt.

Handmade nails all have a roundish cresting head formed by hammer blows, and a square shank that tapers to a fine point. Except in back boards, these hand-wrought nails are seldom found in antique furniture, save in early primitives and large architectural pieces, such as corner cupboards. Cut nails were used with some of the later furniture. They all date before the advent of the machine-made wire nail of about 1870, with its round head and circular shank. When wire nails are found in an antique piece, it shows that it was repaired recently.

Screws as well as nails are a clue to age. The modern screw dates from about 1860. Before that, they were handmade and can be easily recognized. Look at one carefully and you can see that the spiral thread of the shank was hand-cut with a file. As such, it lacks uniformity and is blunt, and the slot in the head was made with a hack saw. It is also irregular and sometimes slightly off center. All handmade screws of iron or brass—for both materials were used—are crude compared to the precisely fashioned machine products.

Hinges

It is well to look at the hinges on table leaves. Those used by old cabinetmakers were also handmade. A blacksmith took a thin strip of wrought iron and bent it double. This left the inner edge rounding enough for the insertion of the pin that united the two parts or leaves. The machine-made iron hinge has leaves stamped from a single thickness of metal and the circular opening for the pin is evenly formed by curling one side of the leaf. Old brass hinges were made by casting the leaves from molten metal; modern ones are machine-stamped from strips of rolled brass. Hence they are much smoother and more even than the cast ones and have the curled edge where the pin joins the two leaves.

For large chests and some dish cupboards, lids and doors were provided with handmade wrought-iron strap hinges, the tip ends of which were frequently given decorative shaping. It is desirable that they should still be on the piece, held in place by wrought-iron nails. Lids of blanket chests, the type with false drawer fronts for the depth of the chest compartment and with one or two drawers beneath, are usually found with pin hinges. These are of hand-wrought iron and are not unlike large cotter pins linked together by inserting one through the eye of the other. They were driven into the wood and made fast by turning over or "clinching" the projecting ends. These blanket chests should, of course, have their original pin hinges. Where leaf hinges are found, they either are replacements of broken pin hinges or indicate that the entire lid may be a replacement.

On certain primitive pieces and those of the early eighteenth century, two other special types of wrought-iron hinges were used, the *butterfly,* so named because the leaves flare outward from the pin and when open have a resemblance to butterfly wings; and the *rat-tail,* most frequently used in pairs on cupboard doors. In the latter, the upper half is a leaf supported by a slender tapering upright curved somewhat like a rodent's tail. Doors of secretaries and dish cupboards were sometimes held in place by variations of the leaf hinge, known as "H" and "L," since they resembled these letters in outline. They were made in both cast brass and wrought iron, though the latter ones were used more for house hardware than for cabinetwork.

Antique furniture equipped with these hinge variations is of greater value because of their presence. Therefore, they should be preserved, and repaired if necessary by a specialist in antique furniture hardware. Some of the large hardware manufacturers are now making assortments of iron hinges and handles that simulate the more elaborate old ones. Smaller sizes of this modern hardware are sometimes used as replacements on antiques. They are displayed by many hardware stores, and once seen will not be mistaken for handmade originals.

Drawer Pulls and Knobs

Comparatively few pieces of antique furniture are found today with their original brasses intact, so replacements are of necessity widely used. They are, naturally, reproductions, and can usually be identified by the way they are held in place. An antique drawer pull of the bail-handle type has posts with hand-filed threads and small cast-metal nuts. In reproductions the threads are die-cut, and the nuts are larger and exactly square. Look for these nuts on the inner side of the drawer where the posts come through from the front.

The same thing can be observed with large brass rosette knobs where the replacements have evenly cut threads and machine-made nuts. In addition to several excellent firms that specialize in accurately designed and carefully made replacement cabinet brasses, some hardware manufacturers produce machine-made stamped brasses that approximate the antique in design but not in workmanship. These are chiefly made for the large furniture factories, but are sometimes used on antiques as replacements. They are always lighter in weight and the posts are held in place by iron screws inserted from the rear. In my opinion these mass-produced brasses so detract from an antique that they should be removed at once and replaced with the more desirable reproductions of the style suited to the piece.

For those antiques originally made with turned button-shaped wooden knobs, measuring from an inch to two and a half inches in diameter, replacements for the missing or broken knob must be used, and most of them are made of mahogany. Original knobs were held in place by hand-filed screws; the new ones are secured by machine-made screws.

Sometimes owners of old pieces tried to bring them up to date in the 1820's and 1830's by removing the brass bail handles in favor of the more fashionable wooden knobs. Usually the outline of the old brasses can be seen on the drawer fronts. Some American Empire chests of drawers have pressed glass knobs secured with metal bolts. No one who has ever seen a set of these old glass pulls in clear, colored or opalescent glass, many of which were made at Sandwich, will ever confuse them with the modern glass knobs that can be bought at almost any hardware store.

A long list of comprehensive books on antique American furniture is available to the collector in the reference section of any large public library. Some deal with furniture of the colonial period; others tell about primitive pieces made of pine; still others suggest how antique furniture may be used in the modern home. It is hard to choose from them, but here are the titles of three books in my own library that I consult frequently: *The Practical Book of Period Furniture,* by Eberlein and McClure, a comprehensive statement of the development of furniture styles from 1600 to 1825 in England, France and America; *American Antique Furniture,* by Edgar G. Miller, Jr., a two-volume work with individual illustrations of about 2,000 different pieces of furniture; and *The Story of American Furniture,* by Thomas Hamilton Ormsbee, which is a case study of what happened to furniture in America from about 1650 to 1840. There is also a ten-cent pamphlet issued by the United States Department of Agriculture, "The Identification of Furniture Woods," by Arthur Koehler, which I have found most helpful.

CHAPTER IV

Old Silver and Its Imitations

Most of the antique silver in the hands of dealers who specialize in this branch of antiques or of those who handle it as an adjunct, is either American or British. Comparatively little is Continental. Therefore, discussion of the chief characteristics of such silver and marks used will be limited to that made by silversmiths of our own country and the British Isles.

Antique pieces of household silver carry one or more marks by which their provenance, age and indentity of individual makers can be established. In the case of English silver, these impressed emblems and ciphers are known as hallmarks, and can be read easily if one understands the significance of each mark in a set. Hallmarks were required by law on English silver.

American silver marks are simpler and do not follow any system required by law. For the most part, each piece

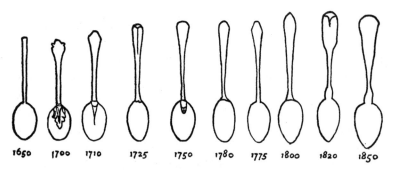

1650   1700   1710   1725   1750   1780   1775   1800   1820   1850

TWO CENTURIES OF AMERICAN SILVER SPOONS
Here are the chief designs of teaspoons from 1650 to 1850. By comparing a spoon with these outline drawings its approximate age can be determined.

bears the mark of its maker. There are some instances where this mark has been omitted; there are others where the mark has been almost totally erased by wear or by reworking a piece. As a random test, I inspected the antique spoons I have. Out of an assortment of sixty-three American-made examples, dating from about 1780 to 1865, I found only two unmarked, and three with marks so faint that they could not be deciphered.

As an example of reworking, I have a beaker made about 1790 that was later converted into a child's mug by the addition of a rococo handle and an allover repoussé decoration showing a country scene. This conversion took place about 1850 and was done by Hammond & Co., New York silversmiths famous for this type of decoration. Their mark on the bottom of the piece almost but not quite obliterates the earlier one of *M M* enclosed in a rectangle. This was the mark of Myer Myers, the famous Jewish silversmith who worked in New York from 1745 to 1795. The mug is a handsome piece and the reworking took place so long ago that it rates as a late antique in its present state, but had it been left as it came from the hands of Myer Myers, its value would be considerably greater.

On American silver the maker's mark might be a single letter, two (or less frequently three) initials, or a name. For example, *D* with a pellet on either side was the mark of Jabez Delano, New Bedford, Massachusetts, 1763-1848; *P S* in a rectangle, that of Philip Syng, Philadelphia, 1676-1739; and *REVERE* in a rectangle was used by the patriot Paul Revere of Boston, 1735-1818. On spoons, such marks are on the back of the handle, either on the shank near the bowl or at the wide upper end. On larger pieces, such as teapots, cream pitchers, sugar bowls, tankards, beakers and porringers, look for the mark on the base or the side.

Near the upper end of the handle was a favorite spot for the old silversmiths to put their mark on tankards and canns, as silver mugs were originally called. Pieces with lids sometimes have two marks, one on the main part and the other on the cover. I have known of a few rare instances, notably a Paul Revere water pitcher that has been in the possession of its present owner's family since 1825, where the mark is inside on the bottom. So if no mark can be found elsewhere on a piece of hollow ware, take a good look inside. A physician's flashlight with plastic tongue depressor is very useful for this since the light flows down the plastic extension and lights up the interior of a piece most effectively.

During the past thirty years, much research has been done in the field of American silver and the craftsmen who made it. As a result names, marks, working years and locations have been recorded for well over 2,500 silversmiths. Such a check list is too long for inclusion here, but may be found in such volumes as *Old Silver,* by Seymour Wyler; *American Silversmiths and Their Marks,* by Stephen G. C. Ensko; and *Marks of Early American Silversmiths* by Ernest M. Currier. For silver made in particular localities, there are also such books as *Maryland Silversmiths,* by J. Hall Pleasants and Howard Sill; *Silversmiths of the State of New York Outside of the City of New York,* by George Barton Cutten; and *South Carolina Silversmiths,* by E. Milby Burton.

All dealers who specialize in silver have these and other authoritative books for reference in their shops, as well as standard ones dealing with European silver. They can also be found in the reference sections of most good-size public libraries.

In addition to these maker's marks, three others are sometimes found on American silver of the mid-nineteenth century, especially on spoons, and help to date such pieces. These marks are "pure coin," "warranted," and sometimes "warranted pure coin." Their use dates from shortly after 1847, the year when Rogers Brothers of Hartford, Connecticut, started the first successful manufactory of plated silver in this country. Made of a base metal and electroplated with silver, such ware looked like silver and sold for much less. Silversmiths, in self-defense and to show the superiority of their products, began marking them in one of these three ways, in addition to their regular touch marks. The mark "pure coin" referred to the centuries-old practice of melting silver coins for use as raw material.

My maternal grandfather, Bradbury M. Bailey, of Rutland, Vermont, was one of these late silversmiths. His working years were from 1852 to 1878. He marked his spoons in various ways—B. M. Bailey; B. M. Bailey, Rutland, Vt.; B. M. Bailey with one of the following additions, "pure coin," "warranted pure coin," or just "warranted." A very few, made just before he closed his silversmithing shop, bear "Sterling" as a designation of quality.

When our large Western mines, such as the Comstock Lode in Nevada, began to produce silver in large quantities, a standard of 925 parts pure silver to 75 parts copper alloy was adopted for commercial silver and has continued ever since. About this time, too, American silversmithing changed from a handcraft to factory production. So, with the few exceptions of spoons obviously made by hand, any silver bearing the sterling mark dates after 1874 and is too late to be considered antique.

Shortly after silver electroplating became commercially successful in the United States, several makers of pewter or Britannia teasets took advantage of this new scientific development and began to plate their hollow ware. Tea and coffee services and related pieces so made are not, by strict interpretation, collectible antiques. But since many people, like myself, possess tea services or single pieces of this sort that have been family keepsakes for many years, a check list of thirty-four of the earlier makers is included in this book as an addenda. It gives the names and dates of these platers of hollow ware, and also those of the chief makers of plated knives, forks and spoons. The majority were located in Connecticut, but Massachusetts, New York and Pennsylvania had a good number, and there were two in San Francisco.

All of this plated ware was marked, either on the back or bottom of each piece, with the maker's name, and either "triple plate" or "quadruple plate" was added as an indication of quality. In a teaset, on the bottom of each piece a number is also frequently found, as, for instance, "1790" on a tea service marked "Rogers, Smith & Co., New Haven, Ct.," which is one of my family possessions. Collectors should be warned that such a number is not, as some wishfully think, the year when it was made. It is merely the style number of the particular design, by which the manufacturer identified it in his illustrated catalogue. For example, my teaset was purchased *new* in 1868 from the Bradbury M. Bailey already mentioned.

Plated tea- and coffeepots made before 1850 have carved wooden handles, usually of maple dyed black to simulate ebony. Metal-handled ones equipped with small mother-of-pearl insulators date between 1850 and 1870. This refinement is not found on cheaper pots or on those of a later date.

Early plated tea and coffee services were usually made in restrained classic urn shapes or in the English or French baroque designs of the eighteenth century. They were never loaded with the allover engraved decoration which came later, along with th widespread vogue for casters, cake baskets, tureens, ewer-shaped water pitchers and goblets without which no prosperous household of the 1870's was properly equipped.

Later the American plated-silver manufacturers outdid even the Victorian, and their designs seemed to have been inspired by about everything, including the kitchen stove or a stable lantern. Most plated silver made after 1870 is not only not collectible; it is not worth harboring unless one wants a few examples to show how bad American taste could be at times and the extremes to which makers went in catering to it.

English silver has one distinct advantage over our own. It is marked much more uniformly and clearly, for each piece bears a set of symbols called hallmarks, which tell where it was made, the year of its making, and the identity and working years of its maker, and that it was assayed for quality of metal.

These hallmarks were so called from the fact that the marking was done first at the guild hall or office in London of the Worshipful Company of Goldsmiths, and later also in government assay offices maintained in London and other principal silversmithing towns of England, Scotland, Wales and Ireland.

The history of English hallmarks goes back at least five hundred years. Books on the subject should be consulted for details and tables of marks. Here, at the risk of oversimplification, just a few cogent highlights are given to indicate what proper reading of a set of marks can tell about a piece. The hallmarks were clearly impressed and are easy to find. They are usually on the side, edge of base, rim or under side of a piece. Knives, forks, spoons and the like are marked on the back of the handle.

As early as 1300 an Act of Parliment required that each piece of silver plate be submitted by its maker to authorities of his guild for marking. Incised with a small steel punch, such marking was proof that the piece was the work of an accredited master silversmith. In 1327, the London Company of Goldsmiths was granted a royal charter. To it were delegated police powers for regulating its members and enforcing purity of metal. Gradually these became a code that governed the silversmithing craft.

By 1478, records show that the Goldsmiths Company adopted a series of three marks that had to be impressed on each piece of silver and done under its supervision. Sale of unmarked silver was illegal and penalities for such black marketing were severe. The marks were a leopard's head (crowned until 1850 and uncrowned after that year), a date letter and the individual device of the maker. The leopard's head was proof that the piece bearing it was the work of a member of the Goldsmiths Company. Later it became the mark designating London-made silver. The date letter, changed annually, recorded the year when a piece was made. The maker's touch was at first a device, such as a key or a fish, taken from the sign that hung over each craftman's shop. The date letters ran through the alphabet, with J, V, W, X, Y and Z omitted because of possible confusion. At the end of each series a new and different design of letter was adopted.

A fourth symbol was added to the set of hallmarks in 1538. This was the lion passant, which in the language of heraldry means "walking lion." It was placed between the date letter and the maker's touch. Like the other three, it is still in use, and always faces left. This lion passant was additional proof that the piece bearing it had been tested for quality and conformed to the legal standard.

After this the individual silversmiths gradually changed their touches from trade-mark-like devices to the first letter of their surnames or to those of their first and last names, mounted on a small shield or other shape. This appears to have become the common practice by 1610. There was no further change in the character of hallmarks until 1697. From then to 1719, a figure of Britannia and a lion's head erased (severed at the neck) replaced the leopard's head and the lion passant to show that the metal used in making pieces so marked contained more pure silver and less alloy than the current English coinage. This was required by a law designed to prevent silversmiths from converting coins into pieces of domestic plate, since this practice had created a serious shortage of metallic currency.

In 1720, use of the leopard's head and the lion passant was revived, but occasional pieces of plate made of silver of greater purity were still marked with the Britannia and lion's head punches. The head of the reigning sovereign, fifth and last punch in a series of hallmarks, was added in 1784, when newly made silverware became subject to a luxury tax. The American Revolution and her other wars had cost England a great deal, and this silver tax was enacted to provide additional revenue. The sovereign's head was inserted in the set of hallmarks between the lion passant and the maker's touch, and continued to be used until 1890, when the excise tax on silverware was repealed.

At first, silver made elsewhere in England was subject to the same regulations and bore the same hallmarks as that produced in London. By about 1565, the earliest of the silvermaking centers outside of London established individual town marks that replaced the leopard's head. By the early seventeenth century there were a total of forty-nine localities in Great Britain and Ireland that had their own distinct town marks. Most of them were never important silver-producing centers and ceased after comparatively short span of activity.

There were, however, six places in England, two in Scotland and two in Ireland where silver was made in sufficient quantity or late enough so that examples bearing their special town marks are likely to be found in American antique shops. They and their town marks were Birmingham, an anchor; Sheffield, a crown; Newcastle, two castles above

| This mark says "Made in London" | This means the year 1796 | Government Assay Office Stamp—for Quality | Sovereign's Head Duty Mark | The Maker's own mark |

TYPICAL ENGLISH SILVER HALL MARKS
Enlarged drawings of a set showing the individual punches and their proper position.

one castle; York, five lions passant on a Greek cross; Chester, the word STERLING until 1700, three lions and three wheat-sheaves until 1778, and since then, three sheaves of wheat and a dagger; Edinburgh, a three-towered castle, and after 1746 the thistle as a separate touch; Glasglow, a complicated oval design consisting of a tree, a bird, a fish and a bell; Dublin, a crowned harp; and Cork, either STERLING or STIRLING. Both variations of spelling were also abbreviated.

Such are the principal facts concerning hallmarks on English silver, reduced practically to an outline. No attempt has been made to deal with the individual marks of even the most outstanding of such craftsmen as Paul Lamerie, or to tell anything about that interesting group of women silversmiths, like Hester Bateman, who flourished in England for over a century. For such details the best source book is *An Illustrated History of English Plate,* by Sir C. J. Jackson, published in London in 1911. It has illustrated tables of these hallmarks, including maker's marks, dates and locations. Easier of access, though not as inclusive, is *Old Silver,* by Wyler, already cited.

Because of the quantities of silver made in England over such a long period, large amounts of it dating between 1760 and 1830 have been imported for some years by our dealers in antique silver. Probably as much more will be brought over in the years to come. Because this silver has been plentiful and prices for it within reason, making copies and then marking them with forged hallmarks has not been as widely practiced as some people believe.

When it has been attempted, the quality of the workmanship, as in most other fakes, is so inferior as to be easily detected by anyone accustomed to handling antique silver. But every so often a good piece of English silver, definitely old, turns up with the genuine mark of a desirable maker, yet is questionable. It is a forgery that can be detected by simply

LONDON HALL MARKS.

Year	Letter	Year	Letter	Year	Letter	Year	Letter	Year	Letter	Year	Letter	Year	Letter
1696		1716	A	1736	a	1756	A	1776	a	1796	A	1816	a
1697		1717	B	1737	b	1757	B	1777	b	1797	B	1817	b
1698		1718	C	1738	c	1758	C	1778	c	1798	C	1818	c
1699		1719	D	1739	d	1759	D	1779	d	1799	D	1819	d
1700		1720	E	1740	e	1760	C	1780	e	1800	E	1820	e
1701	ff	1721	F	1741	f	1761	F	1781	f	1801	F	1821	f
1702		1722	G	1742	g	1762	G	1782	g	1802	G	1822	g
1703		1723	H	1743	h	1763		1783	h	1803	H	1823	h
1704		1724	I	1744	i	1764	J	1784	i	1804	I	1824	i
1705		1725	K	1745	k	1765	k	1785	k	1805	K	1825	k
1706		1726	L	1746	l	1766	L	1786	L	1806	L	1826	l
1707		1727	M	1747	m	1767	M	1787	m	1807	M	1827	m
1708		1728	N	1748	n	1768	n	1788	n	1808	N	1828	n
1709		1729	O	1749	o	1769	O	1789	O	1809	O	1829	o
1710		1730	P	1750	P	1770	P	1790	P	1810	P	1830	p
1711		1731	Q	1751	q	1771	Q	1791	q	1811	Q	1831	q
1712		1732	R	1752	r	1772	R	1792	r	1812	R	1832	r
1713		1733	S	1753	s	1773	S	1793	S	1813	S	1833	s
1714		1734	T	1754	t	1774	T	1794	t	1814	T	1834	t
1715		1735	V	1755	u	1775	U	1795	U	1815	U	1835	u

Later cycles — each of twenty letters as above — commence thus :—

A 1836   a 1856   A 1876   a 1896   a 1916

The date letter is changed on May 29th of each year.

LEADING DATES AND SPECIMEN MARKS.

Description	Year	Marks
1697 (Mch. 27) to 1720 (June I) Higher Standard.	1697	
1720 Old Standard restored.	1721	
1784 to 1890 Sovereign's head (or duty mark) added.	1784	
	1786	
1822 Leopard's head without crown.	1822	
	1837	

—— BRITISH SOVEREIGNS. ——

Anne 1702 ~ George I 1714 ~ George II 1727 ~ George III 1760
George IV 1820 ~ William IV 1830 ~ Victoria 1837 ~ Edward VII 1902-1922

breathing on the hallmark. Moisture generated will bring out the lines of an inlaid piece of silver bearing the hallmark, which was taken from the back of a damaged spoon or similar item and skillfully inserted in a good but unmarked piece.

Since all dealers and many collectors know of this trick, such faking has not been as profitable as it once was, and I doubt if much of this inlay conterfeiting is being done today. Certainly no dealer of reputation knowingly buys or sells such a piece. Consequently the best protection for the average collector is to patronize established dealers whose judgment he respects.

From about 1750 to 1850 a special group of English craftsmen produced hollow-ware pieces, trays and the like, of a less costly material known as Sheffield plate. Today this ware is equally as collectible as silver. In making it, the craftsman started with a small block of copper. Fused to the upper and under sides of it were thinner blocks of silver. By repeatedly passing the block under heavy pressure between polished rollers, it gradually became a thin sheet of metal with silver top and bottom and copper between, in layers like these of the thin plywood so much used today for the sides of large packing boxes. From these sheets Sheffield plate makers fashioned a wide range of graceful table and sideboard pieces, candlesticks and other items that followed the designs of similar silver pieces. The copper core, of course, showed at the edges; and to cover it, silver-wire beading or heavier gadrooning was applied with solder.

Nearly a hundred English makers of Sheffield plate are known. Fifty-one were located in Sheffield, and seventy-four in Birmingham. They continued their work until the easier and less expensive method of electroplating superseded it. Marking Sheffield plate was not required until 1784. After that date, each maker recorded his mark and impressed it on his wares. They were of the trade-mark sort, with maker's name or initials most favored, although small individual punches resembling those of a hallmark were sometimes used. For a check list of these marks, giving makers' names, dates and location, Wyler's *Old Silver* can be consulted once again with profit. The best book dealing solely with this particular subject is *A History of Old Sheffield Plate,* by Frederick Bradbury.

Much of the antique Sheffield plate found today will have considerable copper showing because the silver has been worn away by repeated polishing. The only remedy is to re-plate the entire piece. Objects that have been so restored are not as valuable as those left in original condition, but they have by no means lost all merit as collectible antiques. They have simply been rejuvenated by the only method possible.

There are also reproduction pieces, done within the last thirty or forty years, by electroplating on a base of copper. They are marked "Sheffield" and sometimes bear a maker's name, but should not be confused with antique Sheffield. They are just good usable copies. The only pieces that rate as collectible antiques are those by makers whose names are found in the check lists of old Sheffield-plate craftsmen.

One sometimes finds a piece of antique silver that was repaired years ago by a workman who was either lacking in skill or was unwilling to take the trouble necessary to do a neat job. As a result, an overdose of solder was applied to a handle that had come loose, or a leak was so slathered over with solder as to cover part of the engraved decoration. In buying a piece of old silver, it is usually well to avoid one marred by such sloppy work, though one must expect to see frequent traces of legitimate repairs. These do not affect the value of a piece if skillfully done.

Occasionally, too, one finds pieces that were converted many years ago from one use to another. Transforming tankards into small teapots by cutting a hole in one side and adding a tubular spout was a change frequently made about the middle of the nineteenth century. As a result, the value to present-day collectors of many a fine tankard was reduced to only a quarter of what it would have been otherwise.

There is little the average collector can do for himself in repairing antique silver. For example, taking a dent out of the side of a bowl is not just a simple job of tapping it with a light hammer. It requires skill and a number of special silversmithing tools. Even removing toothmarks and dents from bowls of American coin silver spoons requires more knowledge and skill than the average collector is likely to possess. Too often an amateur in trying to correct a minor blemish on a piece of old silver succeeds only in marring it further. My advice is to do nothing more than polish old silver. Leave all repairs to an expert.

CHAPTER V

Antique Porcelain and Earthenware

Ever since a few Americans began collecting antiques nearly a century ago, china has run a close second to furniture. This is understandable, since these products of the potter's wheel offer a wider variety than any other group of antiques. What one may expect to find in a well-stocked antique shop may be taken as a cross section. It will probably range from crude crocks made by our native "jugtown" potteries to sophisticated tablewares and decorative accessories from the best kilns of Europe and China. These date from about 1750 to the height of the Victorian style, or as late as 1870.

The quantity and quality of dishes possessed by colonial American families varied according to the family's prosperity. All china being fragile, comparatively little dating before 1800 has survived. Moreover, since few American potteries making the finer things for household use produced wares in sufficient quantity to satisfy the demand, most china owned by American families came from abroad, and much of it was made especially for the American market. Some of it, like the historic blue and white Staffordshire and the export china from Canton, was decorated with American views or symbols. Therefore, when the collector goes in search of old china he may expect to be offered pieces from the potteries of England, France, Holland, China, Germany, what was once the Austrian Empire and, to a lesser degree, Spain and Italy.

As regards material, china is divided into two kinds—earthenware and porcelain. In earthenware, the body is formed from one or another of the ordinary clays, similar to those used in brickmaking, over which a dense glaze is applied before firing. Porcelains, whether of Chinese, European or American provenance, are either of kaolin clay or some artificial substitute with a practically transparent glaze.

When in doubt as to whether an old piece of china is porcelain or earthenware, hold it over a strong electric-light bulb. If no light shines through, it is earthenware; if it is translucent, it is porcelain. Transparency varies from that of thin milk-white glass to that where only a trace of light can be seen. This variation depends on the composition of the body material and its thickness. Also the greenish, brownish, bluish or other tone of translucence is of great aid in identifying unmarked porcelain pieces.

There are three types of porcelains—hard paste, soft paste and bone. All hard-paste porcelains are made of kaolin clay and glazed with a felspar solution. Pieces of it are cold

Year Letter	Year Letter
1842 X	1855 E
1843 H	1856 L
1844 C	1857 K
1845 A	1858 B
1846 I	1859 M
1847 F	1860 Z
1848 U	1861 R
1849 S	1862 O
1850 V	1863 G
1851 P	1864 N
1852 D	1865 W
1853 Y	1866 Q
1854 J	1867 T

Month	Letter
January	C
February	G
March	W
April	H
May	E
June	M
July	I
August	R
September	D
October	B
November	K
December	A

Key to English Registry of Design Marks 1842-1867

ENGLISH DESIGN REGISTRY MARK
1842-1867

These are found chiefly on earthenware, but also on pressed glass, plated silver and novelties in wood. Roman numeral in circle is the classification; capital letter at left is for month and figure opposite is for day of month. Figure at bottom indicates the bundle in which such a design registry was filed.

to the touch; the glaze does not scratch; and the colors of underglaze decoration are not absorbed into the bisque. When a piece is chipped, which can happen all too easily, the breaks have a cleavage like those to be seen on flint arrowheads, and the pieces are seldom found with food stains, such as tea or the like.

These hard-paste porcelains were fired at very high temperatures, above 2,400 degrees Fahrenheit. Body and glaze were completely fused, as can be seen if one examines a broken piece. This type of porcelain was made by the Chinese from very early times, and when examples, especially those with cobalt blue underglaze decoration, reached Europe in quantity, early in the seventeenth century, they were admired and eagerly sought after. Soon efforts were made to imitate the Chinese porcelain. These started with the Medici china, produced in Italy during the sixteenth century, and continued with that made at Meissen in 1713, at various French porcelain factories during the eighteenth century, and from about 1745 by such English potteries as Bow, Chelsea, Derby and Worcester.

Practically all of these were soft-paste porcelains with slightly varying artificial compounds of white clay and powdered "frit" (pulverized glass) substituted for the natural kaolin used by the Chinese. The term, soft paste, is used to designate the European attempts to simulate Chinese porcelain; pieces made of it are warmer to the touch, scratch fairly easily, and are slightly porous, and if it is chipped the fractures are not as flakelike as in hard-paste porcelains. Also, in soft-paste porcelains the colors of any underglaze decoration tend to be absorbed into the bisque.

Soft-paste porcelains were fired twice, first unglazed and then after being coated with whatever glazing was used at a particular pottery. Temperatures for firing were about 1,900 degrees Fahrenheit. These porcelains were made in increasing quantities by Continental and English potteries until after discoveries of sizable deposits of kaolin in Saxony, in the south of France and in Cornwall, which took place about 1770. After this, potters gradually changed to the making of hard-paste porcelain.

Bone china, the third type of porcelain, was an English development. It was perfected about 1800 in Staffordshire by Josiah Spode II, son of the founder of the Spode pottery. To the mixture of white clay and felspar he added burned cattle bones. This resulted in a body that was halfway between the hard paste of Chinese origin and the soft paste developed in Europe, and it required but one firing. It was such a practical and economical solution of the porcelain-formula problem that within ten years bone china had become standard with all English potteries. It is translucent, its glaze is free from the hard, glasslike quality of the Chinese product, and it does not chip as easily as either of the other two kinds of porcelain.

The first commercially successful effort to make porcelain in the United States was started in Philadelphia in 1825 by William Ellis Tucker, and was continued after his death in 1832 by his successor, Judge Joseph Hemphill, who carried on the business until 1838. Known as Tucker china, this porcelain, in general appearance as well as in the shape of the pieces, closely resembled the French porcelains of that time. Indeed, this resemblance is so close that a good proportion of the unmarked Tucker pieces have been mistakenly classed as early nineteenth-century French porcelain. Fluted dishes decorated in gold of the design popularly called "wedding band" were one of the standard products of the pottery. Large ornamental vases and handsome pitchers and jugs decorated with sepia landscapes and birds and flowers in natural colors were also made there.

After this short-lived native venture, porcelains sold in the United States were imported for many years. One of the most successful in capturing the American market was Charles

Haviland, who established a porcelain factory at Limoges, France, in 1840. With him and his successors, manufacturing porcelains for sale in America was a primary objective. The reputation of Limoges china became so high in this country that for over sixty years more Haviland porcelains were sold here than those of all other European makers combined.

On fine porcelain tablewares, the colored and gilt decorations were applied after the pieces had acquired their glaze. A second firing at a lesser heat then followed, to fix the decoration. This is known as overglaze decoration and explains why the gold-leaf ornamentation has partially disappeared on many old porcelain dishes. The second firing did not fuse it into the body glaze, so through the years this gold has been washed away.

Porcelain dinner services and large pieces from 1760 on were all decorated by artists who made china painting their life work. Some of the best of these decorators even marked the pieces they ornamented with their names or individual ciphers. Such signed pieces are most desirable.

Beginning about 1875, for greater output and lower cost, porcelain factories used the decalcomania process. Colored decorations lightly printed on paper were dampened and pressed by hand on the surface of the pieces. After the moisture had loosened the design from the paper, the paper was removed and the porcelains were given a second quick firing. Pieces so decorated are, of course, not as fine as the older hand-painted ones. This decalcomania decoration can sometimes be felt if the fingertips are passed over it lightly.

Antique porcelain tablewares and ornamental pieces, except those of Chinese origin, usually bear the mark of the pottery or factory where they were made. Many books that give the individual marks have been written about porcelains. Some are exhaustive works in several volumes, with much more detailed information than the average collector needs or can readily understand. On the reference shelves of most public libraries one or another of the books of marks can be found. Most of them include historical data about each of the potteries or factories. The two reference books on this subject that I have found most helpful are *The Practical Book of Chinaware,* by Eberlein and Ramsdell, and *Marks and Monograms on European and Oriental Pottery and Porcelain,* by William Chaffers. The latter, a monumental English work, is the standard for all others. It has been revised and republished in the United States several times.

In collecting pieces of porcelain, the beginner should study each item carefully. The pottery mark, if present, will help. But not everything was marked, as, for example, the purple luster teasets made in Staffordshire about 1810 and often decorated with flowers or berries done in color. In time, however, one becomes familiar enough with these unmarked porcelains so that it is possible to recognize the work of the different potteries by the difference in amount and tint of translucence. Defects to be observed are chips, age cracks (the darker lines where a piece is partially cracked but still whole) and breaks that have been repaired. Pieces with chips, with age cracks that are not too bad, or those where the decoration has partially disappeared are worth collecting, though naturally they are less valuable than the same ones in mint condition.

In the case of broken pieces that have been mended with cement or rivets, circumstances must govern. For example, a repaired teapot lid does not condemn an otherwise perfect teaset. A Chinese porcelain plate decorated with the emblem of the Order of the Cincinnati that has been repaired with rivets is worth acquiring and will probably cost a hundred dollars or more. Such an item is for the collector's cabinet, but as a rule single pieces of porcelain, badly damaged or broken, are not things to collect or cherish. This is particularly true of tableware, which should be in good enough condition for occasional use at least.

Sometimes a piece of porcelain is found in which some-one—and I suspect it was one of the ladies who painted china as an avocation back in the 1890's—disguised a break or crack with additional free-hand decoration. Such camouflage is not hard to recognize, since the added decoration differs in style and technique from the original. Also, the line of a concealed break or crack can be easily seen by looking at the back of a plate or inside a teapot, cream pitcher or sugar bowl.

In practically all pieces of porcelain repaired by even skilled professionals, what has been done will stand out clearly when the piece is held before a strong electric light. This test will also disclose spots where "china filler" has been used to replace missing bits or chips, for such filler is opaque. Spouts and handles of teapots, coffeepots and cream pitchers; handles and knobs of sugar bowls and covered dishes; and minor parts, especially hands of figurines, should be well examined for repairs of this sort.

Although reputable dealers try to check for repairs of this kind all pieces of porcelain they handle, and sell the china accordingly, now and again a minor restoration or an unusually well-done repair can be overlooked. Therefore the collector should make his own inspection also. If anything is found that looks as if it might be a repair or restoration, do not hesitate to point it out to the dealer and ask his opinion.

In figurines and large ornamental pieces, small breaks, such as a missing finger, are not too bad blemishes; but a missing arm or a shattered and restored base certainly does not enhance the value of such pieces. The collector should make his own inspection and, realizing what toll the years have taken, buy accordingly.

Although porcelain was always the finer material, many beautiful and highly desirable examples of old china were of earthenware. These are always opaque, since they were made of a native dense clay, but don't discard a piece just because it is not translucent. Josiah Wedgwood, England's greatest potter, never made any porcelain, although the Wedgwood pottery did so for a brief time after his death. All of his beautiful and much sought-after basalt and jasperware ornamental pieces and his fine queen's ware dinner services were earthenware of fine grade and were fashioned with great skill and artistic merit.

The basalt and jasperware that he began making about 1770 at his Etruria pottery in Staffordshire are among the ceramic objects that have long appealed to collectors. The restrained classic beauty of the basalt pieces and the exquisite modeling of white relief figures and groups on jasperware, many of them modeled by the able English artist, John Flaxman, make these old Wedgwood pieces true works of art as well as original antiques.

Specimens of both wares are available, since they were produced in surprising quantities. Each bears an incised mark on base or back that makes identification easy and sure. Until 1780, the year his London partner, Thomas Bentley died, the mark was WEDGWOOD AND BENTLEY, and after that just WEDGWOOD. Over a generation ago the Wedgwood potteries (still owned by descendants of its founder) revived the making of both basalt and jasperware, using the old dies and molds. These new pieces bear the incised mark, WEDGWOOD, and when exported to the United States "MADE IN ENGLAND" is likewise incised.

None of these products of Wedgwood's Etruria pottery should be confused with copies, especially in jasperware, made in Germany in the late 1920's. These can be detected through the colors of the background. Usually light blue or a pale olive green, they are pale and washed out when compared with a Wedgwood original. Also the outlines of the white figures in low relief are blurred, never sharp as they are on real Wedgwood. That they are late and poor copies will be confirmed by the absence of the incised Wedgwood mark. Yet I have found neophyte collectors in some sections of the Middle West who were mistakenly collecting these copies of German origin.

Highly desirable are the Toby jugs by Whieldon and the historical figures by Ralph Wood. The same is true of the American historic blue and white dishes made in Staffordshire by a number of potters from about 1815 to 1850, or the much earlier blue and white plates, vases and tiles produced in the Netherlands at Delft.

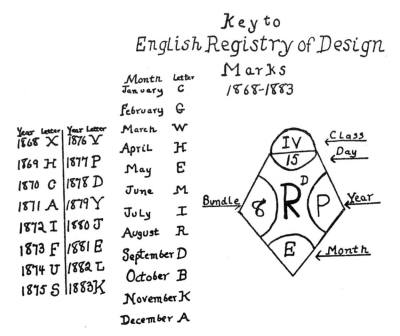

Key to
English Registry of Design
Marks
1868-1883

Month	Letter
January	C
February	G
March	W
April	H
May	E
June	M
July	I
August	R
September	D
October	B
November	K
December	A

Year Letter		Year Letter	
1868	X	1876	V
1869	H	1877	P
1870	C	1878	D
1871	A	1879	Y
1872	I	1880	J
1873	F	1881	E
1874	U	1882	L
1875	S	1883	K

ENGLISH DESIGN REGISTRY
1868-1883

There has been a change in the placing of the different symbols. The year letter is at the right; the month at the bottom; the day immediately beneath the classification numeral; the bundle number opposite the year letter. The maker's name was never included in either of these registry marks. To obtain this, send a careful drawing of mark and a fee of one shilling to the Comptroller, the Patent Office, London, England. Allow about two months for a search and report.

Some collectors refer to china made of the native clays as faience. The history of its making in England and on the Continent goes back a long way. It received great stimulus when the first explorers and East India merchants began to bring back blue and white dishes from China. Efforts to copy them resulted in the faience pieces made in England and on the Continent from about 1700 with decorations that simulated the Chinese, done in a dense white glaze. Other colors were also used, and some of the pieces were made of one or another type of stoneware. Most of the books dealing with china made of native clays are limited to consideration of the work of one country, one locality or individual potteries. Beginning well before 1815 and continuing until about 1860, English potters, especially those of Staffordshire, came close to having a monopoly on earthenware table dishes, toilet sets and decorative items supplied to the people of the United States. Many books have been published in the past twenty years or so regarding these potters and what they made for the American market, and scarcely any public library is without one or more. Almost any one of them will provide a good working knowledge of this kind of antique English china.

In many ways the most attractive to the average collector, as well as the most easily recognized, is the historic blue and white. It was a transfer ware, that is, the decorations were transferred from engraved copper plates by printing them on sheets of paper and then pressing them on the dry but unglazed unfired clay. After the clay had absorbed the design the paper was removed, and each piece was dipped in a glazing solution and then fired. The under-glaze-decorated pieces that are of a rich indigo blue with the design impression sharp and clear are the most desirable. Those in a "flowing" blue or a pale shade about that of "baby blue" are later and less collectible. Blue, however, was not the only color used by Staffordshire potters. Pieces of same age can be found in

CARE AND REPAIR OF ANTIQUES

pink, sepia, black, purple, green, gray, mulberry and brown. Some are even in two colors.

After the vogue for blue and white china passed, its place was taken by a number of different designs or by white undecorated ironstone. Much of this ware bears the mark of its originator and reads: "Mason's Patent Ironstone China." A considerable quantity was also made by other English potters and marked *Ironstone,* either with or without their names. Ironstone was a heavier ware, the shapes were in the Victorian style and the knobs of covers were frequently in the shapes of fruits or vegetables of the melon sort. Platters and covered dishes were usually oval; teapots and larger pitchers were sometimes eight-sided and flared downward. Until recently ironstone did not have much appeal for collectors because of its thickness and weight, but it is now popular for use in country homes or those furnished in the Victorian style. As a result, prices for ironstone have risen sharply.

Along with this tableware, small Staffordshire pieces, Victorian in flavor, such as figurines, larger mantel pieces shaped to represent romantic castles or sentimentally appealing cottages, men and women on horseback, and a wide variety of dogs, especially primly sitting spaniels, are very popular with collectors.

In acquiring earthenware pieces, one should watch for about the same repairs and restorations as with porcelains, but they are not as easily seen, since the ware is opaque. So far as I know, there have been no counterfeits of these dishes produced in quantity. This cannot be said for the Staffordshire figurines and larger ornamental pieces. A few years ago, faking them was a standard business with some of the smaller potteries in Czechoslovakia, and many of these copies still crop up in second-hand stores and shops of less experienced antique dealers. The Japanese also made their share of these fakes, favoring the smaller figurines. Most of

these counterfeits can be recognized by the poor quality of
the modeling and the carelessness with which colors were
applied, as well as by the inferiority of the glaze. In the larger
human figures and the dogs, modeling was much less distinct
and the colors were not handled with the same directness. It
is a good rule to question any of these ornamental pieces that
are not clear cut, are of poor colors or have rough and crude
glaze.

On some of these figurine fakes, the country-of-origin
mark can be found imprinted beneath the glaze on the under
side of the base. More frequently it has been removed by
grinding on an emery wheel or by some other abrasive. This
also removes the glaze and leaves a telltale rough spot. Sometimes an effort to conceal this has been made by touching the
rough spot with a colorless varnish or lacquer, but this can
also be seen if one looks closely enough. Where fake figurines
are decorated with gold, silver or purple luster stripes or
other touches, the work is much brighter than that on the
genuine.

The native American pottery pieces of interest to collectors are mostly crocks, pickle jars and jugs, made in many
small potteries that flourished in various parts of the country
from a little after 1800 to 1880. Many of them bear potters'
marks which can be identified by consulting such specialized
books as *American Potters and Pottery,* by John Ramsey.
These homely items were mostly of redware, the glaze of
which often had decorative black splotches, of brown glazed
wares, and of stonewares in gray and black. Some bore hastily
done slip decorations, but a few pieces had intricate and carefully incised ornamentation that included names and dates.

There were also some potteries, such as those at Bennington, Vermont, East Liverpool, Ohio, and South Amboy, New
Jersey, that produced fine pieces in a brown mottled glaze,
generally known as Rockingham. These potteries also made

some very fine animal figures, especially deer, lions and barn-yard cattle, which are rarities now.

Among the Pennsylvania Dutch, there was a long line of skilled potters who made about everything from pie plates to delightful, small animal figures and graffito examples, in which the decoration was achieved by scratching through the lighter colored slip glaze to the dark red of the body. Some-times an additional slip of another color was used for contrast. Some of the Pennsylvania potters worked until about 1930, but their late pieces generally lack the directness of earlier examples.

There have been a few scattered efforts to make dupli-cates of these early American potteries in quantity for the gift-shop trade. Luckily what was produced so faintly re-sembles the originals that anyone with any feeling for an-tiques will not be deceived.

CHAPTER VI

American Glass—Pressed and Blown

Although glass was the first American industry, with the first glasshouse dating back to 1609 at Jamestown, Virginia, that found in average antique shops is of middle and late nineteenth-century production. Eighteenth-century blown glass made at the furnaces of Caspar Wistar of South Jersey, Henry William Stiegel at Manheim, Pennsylvania, and John Frederick Amelung at New Bremen, Maryland, rates among the rarest of American antiques. Early nineteenth-century blown glass also rates as very rare.

What is available to collectors in the main is pressed glass and late blown pieces. Such glass dates considerably after 1825, when Deming Jarves, using an iron mold, produced a pressed-glass water tumbler at Sandwich, Massachusetts. This process of mechanically forcing molten glass into a mold of carefully executed design, spread from there. Soon it was employed by numerous glass factories, which first centered around Pittsburgh, Pennsylvania, and then extended westward to Zanesville and other points in Ohio and elsewhere.

By shortly after 1850, Sandwich and the Western factories were making entire table services of what we now know as pattern glass. This type of glass continued to be made right up to the closing years of the century. It included table settings in fully five hundred different patterns and many more designs produced as individual pieces.

Before 1931, comparatively few collectors were interested in pattern glass; the subject was all too confused. Then *Early American Pressed Glass,* by Ruth Webb Lee, appeared. This book classified and named patterns and listed the pieces known to have been made in the numerous designs. With order and a plan thus provided for them, collectors in all parts of the country found a new interest, and they began assembling table settings in the patterns that most appealed to them. To use a well-worn American phrase, it swept the country. Dealers and collectors specializing in this decorative and varied glassware increased and multiplied until there are now more of them than of all others in the antiques field combined. Even old die-hards who at first dismissed it contemptuously as "just a fad of the depression," now realize that the collecting of pattern glass has come to stay and will probably remain a leader.

As certain patterns increased in popularity, they became correspondingly scarce and costly. This proved tempting to the faker and counterfeits appeared, though not in entire table settings. Making all the molds needed for such a venture called for too large an investment; rather, individual pieces, such as goblets, tumblers, plates and compotes in one or another of the most popular patterns were counterfeited.

They were apparently made on order for some unscrupulous peddlers, without a definite plan of action. A goblet in one pattern, a plate in another would suddenly appear in the shops of less experienced dealers, the goblet being the piece most copied. Some of the best-known patterns in which fake goblets have appeared are "Daisy and Button," "Ruby Thumbprint," "Lion," "Westward-Ho," "Paneled Grape," "Three-Face," "Pleat and Panel," "Cherry," "Rose-in-Snow," "Moon and Star," "Wildflower" and "New England Pineapple."

Although these fakes do not look too bad at first glance, distinct points of variance from the originals can be seen on closer inspection. Since the molds in which these copies were pressed were not cut with the same care as those of the originals, design details do not stand out with the same sharpness. Moreover the material is the newer and cheaper lime glass instead of the earlier lead glass. A piece of lime glass when tapped with a pencil gives off a dull tone; one of lead glass has a bell-like ring, similar to that of blown glass but not as high in pitch.

Distributors of these pattern glass fakes by no means had it all their own way. As early as 1938, Mrs. Lee's *Antique Fakes & Reproductions* was published, in which she described and illustrated current counterfeits and the points at which they varied from the originals. A supplement appeared two years later, and complete revision of this work is now under way.

There are also some patterns of glass tableware that have been made fairly recently, with no intent to copy the old; these should not be confused with somewhat similar designs found in Mrs. Lee's initial book or in her *Victorian Glass*.

Prices of pieces in the ten most popular patterns— "Bellflower," "Horn of Plenty," "Rose-in-Snow," "Wild Flower," "Thousand-Eye," "Three-Face," "Lion," "Westward-Ho," "Milkwhite Blackberry" and "Daisy and Button" —and some others have now reached such high figures that beginners might think collecting pattern glass is too expensive for them. On the contrary, Mrs. Lee informs me that there are still two or three hundred patterns that are just as good and just as interesting, in which pieces can be bought at reasonable prices by those who will take the trouble to look for them.

Between the time that Jarves of the Boston & Sandwich Glass Company made his first pressed-glass tumbler and the time when his factory turned to pattern glass, there was a lapse of nearly thirty years. It was during this period that the lacy Sandwich was produced, long the aristocrat of machine-made glass. Its designs and the silvery quality of its stippled background are what give it the beauty that appeals so much to collectors. It was always made of reasonant lead glass and there have been only a few very poor and easily detected counterfeits. Examples of lacy Sandwich rank among the expensive items of antique glass. Collectors should be careful not to acquire pieces that are badly chipped or that have been ground down and polished to eradicate either a large chip or a bad break.

Glass somewhat similar to lacy Sandwich was produced during the same period at Baccarat, France, but the designs used there were distinctly different. These are illustrated in Mrs. Lee's excellent book, *Sandwich Glass.*

Along with lacy Sandwich, the Boston & Sandwich Glass Company and a number of other houses made a distinct type of glass tableware between 1820 and about 1840 that is now called blown three-mold, so named from the method of its making. A charge of molten glass on the end of a blowpipe was inserted into a hinged mold. The glass worker blew until the charge expanded to the point where the mold design was impressed on it. Then the mold was opened and the object, still attached to the blowpipe, was removed for finishing in the manner customary with blown glass. Designs were mostly geometric, since this mold-blown glass was primarily intended as a less expensive substitute for Irish and English cut glass, then being imported into the United States.

Decanters, goblets, wine glasses, sugar bowls, jars, plates, bowls, tumblers (including flip-glass size), celery vases, salt cellars and sirup jugs were among the principal pieces made for table use. Other items included inkwells, lamps and miniature pieces. Blown three-mold examples are desirable, but expensive and can occasionally be found in antique shops. The best detailed discussion of this type of glass can be found in *American Glass,* by George S. and Helen Mc-Kearin. This comprehensive volume includes over a hundred and twenty-five line drawings of design elements of this mold-blown glass.

There has been a small amount of counterfeiting in this field also, but such fakes can nearly always be identified by two tests. The copies are distinctly heavier than the originals, and if the fingers are passed over the inner surface, that of a copy will be smooth; with an original, ridges and hollows corresponding to the design of the exterior will be felt. In choosing examples of mold-blown glass, the collector should be alert for partial cracks, known as heat checks. These are apt to occur when a piece is subjected to too great changes in temperature.

A collector of my acquaintance had several pieces of such glass displayed in a window on shelves made for the purpose. One winter night the thermometer dropped to a record low of thirty degrees below zero. The next morning he found most of his choice pieces marred in this way, due to the intense cold.

Stoppers of decanters should fit snugly and correspond in design. In the case of a dome-covered sugar bowl, the glass of both cover and bowl should be like in texture, color and tint. If not, it is an assembled piece, consisting of a stray bowl and an odd cover that happened to be of the same size.

At the time American glass factories were making the pattern-glass table settings already commented on, they were also producing some very interesting candlesticks, lamps and vases by the same method. They were made in clear and colored glass and sometimes of two contrasting colors. The semi-opaque white and pastel shades were used. Most of the lamps were designed for whale oil and had the two-tube circular burners used with that fluid. A large proportion of the candlesticks were of the dolphin type. Some of the later lamps with flat kerosene-oil wicks and glass shades were made in pairs as mantel decorations. Vases were also fashioned for this purpose, some with pressed-glass bases and blown-glass containers. All are highly collectible antiques and command high prices.

A considerable number of whale-oil lamps have been reproduced for the interior decorator trade. These copies are not as well shaped and the quality of glass is different and heavier. Candlestick copies are all of the dolphin design. They are of a poorer quality of glass than antique examples, being about that of window glass. Also, they were apparently cast in a single mold; in the originals the candle holder was always made separately and fused to the base. This joining can be seen, and it will be noted that the seams or mold marks are not in perfect alignment. If the lower side of the base is examined carefully, another clue will be found in the fine scratches that go in all directions on the surface. A copy either has none of these or, if any, they are parallel because they have been put there with a file or an emery wheel.

Colorful Victorian ornamental pieces are another type of American glass found in antique shops. These are mostly small vases, fancy baskets, pitchers and similar items. Usually they have handles or applied ornaments done in clear glass or in a contrasting color. Except for such large and ornate objects as epergnes, they are not expensive. Collecting them began only a few years ago.

More expensive, and collected for a much longer time, are glass paperweights. These ball- or bun-shaped pieces all have highly decorative arrangements of colored glass embedded in a clear glass casing. Some are of flowers, fruits or butterflies. Others are mosaic patterns formed of short pieces of multi-colored glass rods and are known as millefiori weights.

These paperweights were imported from France, England and Bohemia. They were also made by skillful craftsmen working at such American factories as the New England Glass Company of Cambridge, Massachusetts; the Boston & Sandwich Glass Company; the Gillerland factory in Brooklyn, New York; and the factory at Millville, New Jersey, where Ralph Barber, who worked as late as 1905, made his Millville rose paperweights. These are the most prized of American weights, and a fine example is considered cheap at a hundred and fifty dollars or more. A good book about these highly specialized items is *Old Glass Paperweights,* by Evangeline H. Bergstrom. It is well illustrated with over a hundred plates, twenty of them in color.

Because of their small size and high value, and because a skilled glass blower needs little more than a spirit lamp to fashion the colored decoration before it is "cased," a good many instances of individual fake weight-making have been discovered. The poorest of these are some bunlike mosaic weights and some floral ones, made in China during the early 1930's. They can be recognized by the low quality of the casing glass, which in some examples has the greenish cast common to beer or soft-drink bottles. These bases are also left rough and creased instead of being ground and polished. Collecting paperweights is fascinating, but one should first see and study representative examples of genuine weights until perfectly familiar with their workmanship and superior colors.

American historical flasks and early squat bottles, made mostly in the eighteenth century, appeal to a number of glass collectors, principally men. Most of the historic flasks were made from about 1810 to 1860. Their decorations include portraits of military and political heroes, portrayals of notable events, and Masonic emblems. They are to be found in a wide range of shapes, sizes and colors. Rare examples are anything but cheap, but other interesting ones can still be bought in many shops at fair prices. The McKearin book, already mentioned, has two chapters on bottles and flasks, which contain perhaps the most concise information available.

About 1925 to 1930 some counterfeit flasks were made, but they are now well known. Among these fakes are the house-shaped "Booze" bottle, a "Success to the Railroad" flask, and two calabash-shaped bottles, one with a profile head of

Washington, with "Father of His Country" lettered above, the other with a full-face bust of Jenny Lind, with her name lettered above, and "Fislerville Glass Works" beneath. Other fakes are a flask with a cornucopia on one side and a basket of flowers on the other; a pint-sized one with a profile of Washington, lettered "The Father of His Country" on both sides, for which no original is known; and a half-pint size with a horse and cart, lettered "Railroad" above and "Lowell" beneath, and having a spread eagle on the reverse. There are also a tall, square, house-shaped bottle, a counterfeit of the Plantation Bitters bottle that lacks the lettering of the original, and a number of copies of the large eight-sided pickle bottles with gothic-shaped panels. Made for the gift-shop trade to serve as lamps bases, these are of heavier glass, which lacks the distinct greenish cast of the originals.

In the days when it was good manners to drink tea from a saucer, many glass cup plates were made. Their patterns ranged from portraits of distinguished Americans and records of events to floral and geometric motifs. Serious collecting of these cup plates is a highly specialized endeavor, and very rare examples bring stiff prices. A few examples, however, add interest to any American glass collection. Some genuine ones that rate as "common" can be bought reasonably.

Cup plates have also been copied, but in only a few designs. Most of these were made to sell as novelties by dealers in modern glass, and are not exact as to design details. All are of the dull-sounding lime glass. Among the few that rate as fakes, are the Bunker Hill design in which the drapery element lacks tassels; a Henry Clay profile facing left, with smaller lettering and faint border design; a butterfly with six-petaled flowers on the border; a steamboat design, with "Benjamin Franklin" in plain lettering and lacking the walking beam over the paddle wheel; and a plain-centered cup plate with the thirteen-heart border but with a plain rim on the base instead of one in rope form.

There is also one of modern production that is sometimes mistaken for an old cup plate. In the center is a full-face head of Washington. Beneath in the border is a facsimile of his signature and his dates, 1732-1799. The rest of the border has thirteen clear stars on a stippled background. There is no known original of like design. Occasionally old cup plates of slightly different designs are discovered. Most of them have been found in the Middle West, where the custom of drinking tea from the saucer continued for some years after it went out of fashion in the East.

Another type of glass sometimes confused with the antique is the hand-blown Mexican. Made in the old tradition in various Mexican villages, considerable quantities have been imported for several years and widely sold here in the decorative sections of department stores and in gift and art shops. Now and then some of it turns up in the smaller antique shops. It comes in blue, aquamarine, olive green and medium brown. The more common pieces are tumblers in various sizes, small wine glasses, pitchers ranging from miniature to the two-quart size, plates from six to ten inches in diameter, covered sugar bowls, plain bowls in a number of sizes and various bottles, including one of a nun in her habit.

This Mexican glass is pleasing and goes quite well with genuine antiques, but differs decidedly from antique South Jersey blown glass. Neither shapes nor colors are the same, and it has a different feel that can be detected by anyone who has handled pieces of genuine Wistar type of glass.

CHAPTER VII

Pewter, Brass and Copper

Antique pewter collecting, like Gaul, is divided into three parts; in this case, American, English and Continental. American-made pewter, for which there is keen demand for well-marked pieces in good condition by a small group of ardent collectors, is simple in shape and ornamentation. Plates, basins, bowls and platters of English pewter frequently have a molding-like edge that approaches the gadrooning found on silver, and some of the circular pieces have serrated rims. Continental pewter items are still more elaborate in form and decorative detail. Among these may be found the wine reservoir with faucet, designed to be hung on the wall, and other pieces that approach the architectural.

Graduated sets of beer and wine measures usually made in baluster shapes, somewhat like domed tankards, may be either English or Continental. This holds for small pieces, such as snuff, tobacco or patch boxes and spectacle bases, with the probability that those with allover engraved decorations are Continental.

A theory is sometimes advanced that Continental pewter is of superior quality because of a percentage of silver. This is just wishful thinking, for all pewter is an alloy of tin, copper and antimony, with some lead added when used to make trinkets. The brightness of this pewter is probably due to years of good care and frequent polishing.

Buyers of English and Continental pewter are mostly collectors who want pieces for decorative effect, although a few have well-selected collections that are representative of the craftsmanship of some particular country.

American pewter, with which most collectors in the United States are concerned, is divided into three periods. They are the pre-Revolutionary, the middle period, and the Britannia or "coffeepot" era. All pewter made here before 1775 is scarce and high-priced, for obvious reasons. Being a soft alloy, pieces that received hard usage were worn out in a few years. Then, during the American Revolution, patriotic families gave liberally of their household pewter to be melted and made into bullets.

During the middle period, which included the last decade of the eighteenth and the first thirty years of the nineteenth centuries, pewterers, located chiefly in Massachusetts, Rhode Island, Connecticut, New York and Pennsylvania, produced quantities of household pewter wares. It is largely examples of their work that are collected today.

Pewter of the Britannia years is not considered as desirable, although some very good pieces were produced then. Among them were teapots, lighting devices and communion services, in which the designs were simple, direct and restrained. This period runs from about 1835 to 1850 or, with the very few pewterers who worked in the Middle West, even as late as 1860. Sellew and Company of Cincinnati, for example, made a number of whale-oil lamps and candlesticks. Their place of business still stands and has been used for many years as an antique shop. Not long ago I saw a pewter collection in Decatur, Illinois, that included several pairs of Sellew candlesticks, all of distinctive and artistic shapes.

This period, which coincided with the time when coffee first started to compete with tea as a table beverage in America, has been called the "coffeepot" era because, with the demand for larger containers in which to serve this fragrant drink, pewterers started making pots ranging in size from eight to twelve or even fourteen inches tall. Unfortunately, the designs for them were inferior to those of earlier or even contemporary teapots, and as the Victorian years advanced they became a little too ornate.

Plates from six to fifteen inches in diameter, basins from six to twelve inches, two- to six-inch porringers, mugs, beakers, tankards with either flat or domed tops, teapots, pitchers up to the two-quart size, platters, tureen ladles, whale-oil and betty lamps, as well as objects for bedroom use were made by our craftsmen during the "good" middle period. There were about seventy-five of these pewterers, and then, as earlier, the craft was frequently followed by two or more members of the same family. Often they were father and son, brothers, or uncles and nephews.

Among these were members of the Boardman family, originally of Hartford, Connecticut, who also worked in Philadelphia and New York. Five different touch marks are known for their pewter. More numerous were the Danforths, who were related to the Boardmans. They originated in Norwich, Connecticut, but worked in Hartford, Middletown and Rocky Hill. Thomas Danforth III (1756-1840) moved from Rocky Hill to Philadelphia to take charge of a branch pewter shop his father had established there. He returned to his Connecticut home town in his old age and died there in 1840. Joseph Danforth II, son of Joseph of Middletown, also left his home state and established a shop in Richmond, Virginia. Eleven different marks are known for this Danforth pewter.

There was also the Bassett family of New York. They worked in both the colonial and middle periods and stayed steadfastly in their native city. The first of these pewterers were Francis Bassett, who died in 1758, and John, who survived him by only three years. They were followed by Francis II and Frederick, who was eleven years younger. Both men died in 1800. All together, these four Bassetts used some ten different marks.

Beginning with Joseph Copeland of Chuckatuck, Virginia, who worked before 1691 and of whose pewter the sole survivor is a marked spoon, the identity, working years and touchmarks of more than a hundred and fifty American pewterers have been studied intensively and have been subjects for books, as well as magazine articles and museum bulletins, for at least thirty years. The best book to date is *Pewter in America,* by Ledlie I. Laughlin, published in 1940. It is in two volumes, and its illustrations include full-size reproductions of all known marks.

Although a few spoons bearing marks of known pewterers are occasionally found, the great bulk are unmarked. This is because they were largely the work of traveling tinkers who went about the country on foot, carrying their molds with them. In this way broken or worn-out pewter was thriftily melted and made into spoons at little cost. Today collectors and dealers who have such molds and pieces of pewter that are beyond repair sometimes repeat this spoon-making process. As a result, pewter spoons of the old shapes but in mint condition, are not hard to buy and are generally inexpensive.

The one out-and-out pewter fake that I have seen is a spoon with a nearly circular bowl and a straight flaring handle. It bears on its back in block letters the mark P R in a square, and is attributed to Paul Revere, the patriot silversmith. Although that versatile man had many occupations, including that of tooth extractor, careful research fails to disclose any evidence that he worked in pewter. The mold used for making the spoon in question was an old brass one, which the faker embellished with these two initials.

Although not to be classed as counterfeits, electroplated pieces that have been stripped of their silver plate are sometimes offered by inexperienced dealers or by rummage and second-hand shops as examples of old American pewter. Such pieces are generally tea- and coffeepots, creamers, sugar bowls, spoon holders, water pitchers, mugs and trays. By wear, repeated polishings or by dipping in an acid bath, every trace of silver has disappeared. Since the white metal base used in making electroplated pieces is an alloy similar to pewter, the error is understandable. However, their shapes are wrong. They are Victorian and frequently have an engraved decoration. Moreover, by a glance at the bottom of such a piece, one will find the mark of one of the American companies that made this plated ware, such as "1847 Rogers Brothers."

The reverse of this sometimes happens—that is, a piece of antique American pewter that was modernized many years ago by silver plating. Once, at a country antiques show in New Jersey, I bought a communion flagon for two dollars that bore the mark of Roswell Gleason of Dorchester, Massachusetts, one of the desirable American pewterers of the middle and late periods. Because it was silver-plated no one had troubled to turn it over and look at the touchmark on the base, so it was a "sleeper" and sold at a low price.

Less easily identified was a domed tankard, now in a large collection of American pewter, by William Will of Philadelphia, who made the pewter inkstand used when the Declaration of Independence was signed. This tankard is a fine piece in mint condition. Its present owner found it one winter in a Florida shop. The silverplating had so dimmed the touchmark that it could scarcely be seen, even with a good glass, but he bought it and then paid nearly as much more to have it stripped expertly so that the pewter underneath would not be acid-pitted.

"From its shape and proportions and the style of thumbpiece, I was certain it was a Philadelphia piece dating before 1775, so I took a chance that it would have a good mark when stripped," its owner remarked as he returned the tankard to its place of prominence in a corner cupboard filled entirely with pewter. "I was just lucky that it turned out to be a William Will piece."

Collectors, in buying pewter, would do well to remember that during the years between World Wars I and II, many of the shops in England and on the Continent sold American tourists new pewter pieces as souvenirs that copied or approximated the old in shapes and designs. Small porringers that could be used as ash trays were very popular, as were mugs in standard and children's sizes. With the time that has elapsed, some of these pieces now look old and well used. Most of them bear no maker's touch and, having been bought abroad, no country-of-origin mark; therefore they are hard to place and date. However, the shapes differ enough so that they should not be confused with antique, unmarked American pewter.

In the search for pewter, do not be too rigid about taking only pieces that are unblemished and on which a maker's touch can be clearly seen. Originally, pewter, both here and abroad, was for everyday use. Being a soft alloy, pieces became bent and even developed holes. Then, after being stored away unused for years, such pieces gathered a dull, lead-like surface. That is the condition of most old pewter when dealers acquire it and so most of it remains, unless it is in the stock of a dealer who specializes in pewter or in the possession of a collector of pewter. Cleaning and polishing pewter takes skill and time. Many dealers don't know how to do it properly, and they also lack the time required.

So the pewter usually stays so dull and discolored that the maker's mark is faint and sometimes illegible. This suits the real pewter collector. He finds it a challenge to his judgment about various pieces. Can a certain tankard be mended without harming its value as a collectible? How keen is his eye in spotting and identifying the obscured marks on a six-inch plate? Can the scale on another be removed, or is it too deeply embedded?

About ten years ago I saw a large circular plate hanging in the shop of a man who mainly did furniture repairing.

He knew nothing about the plate except that it came with some furniture he had bought, which had been stored for years in a woodshed attic. I took the charger down. It was discolored but not corroded. There was a small hole in the rim for the wire by which it had been hung. Held up to the light, I could see no holes where dents had pierced the metal. Then I turned it over, and although no maker's mark was visible I could see traces of hammer marks whereby the plate had been struck up. It was of unusually large size, measuring twenty-two inches in diameter. So I bought it for under ten dollars. When I got it home I cleaned and polished the upper side and used it for several years as a coffee-table top.

Although at times I thought I could see what might be a maker's touch, it was a mark unknown to me. One day an acquaintance particularly interested in English pewter studied it. In the course of an hour, during which he used up two typewriter erasers, he "raised" the mark and cleaned it enough so it could be identified. It was that of Sir John Fryers, who was master of the London Company of Pewterers from 1695 to 1703. Later the curator of an historic house museum pestered me until I sold him that salver for more than ten times what it cost me. I now regret that I let it go. The money is spent, and I doubt if I'll ever again find the plate's equal for size, age or condition.

Although buying pewter so dull and tarnished that its complexion is similar to that of a dirty blackboard usually has a happy outcome, one should be wary of pieces that show signs of serious corrosion. This could be the result of being stored in a place where it was damp, such as a cellar or a shed with a leaking roof, or, if a plate, being used under a potted plant. Such corrosion can be so extensive that even after skilled treatment with an acid bath or by buffing, the surface is badly pitted. There are likely to be fine pinholes, too, where the corrosion has gone through the metal.

A piece so disfigured is not worth over a quarter of what it would be if in average condition; I know from experience. I have a sixteen-inch plate by Simon Edgell, who worked in Philadelphia from 1713 to 1742. It is well marked with his name and bird touch, and would be desirable and rare if in average condition. As it is, I do not value it at over what I paid for it, which was nothing plus five dollars, the cost of having it cleaned as a chance experiment that it might not be as seriously damaged as the surface indicated.

While some pieces of pewter that have the American look are unmarked, more are touched with the maker's mark. The places where these touchmarks are usually found are the under side of plates; the bottom of teapots, tankards and other hollow pieces; the back of the handle of spoons and ladles; and the bottom or the handle of porringers. They were not always clearly impressed, and consequently there are instances where only part of a mark can be seen, even after the piece has been thoroughly cleaned and polished.

When hunting for old pewter, go equipped with a good pocket magnifying glass and an ink eraser. With a few strokes of the latter, one can soon bring out enough of a mark so it can be identified, at least tentatively. Detailed discussion of these American marks would take too long here, but, briefly, with few exceptions they all include the pewterer's name or initials. Many also have a trade-mark-like decorative device, the most used being an eagle, either spread or poised in flight, or an adaptation from the coat of arms of the state where the maker worked. Some others consist of a straight band of four squarish touches that resemble English hallmarks. Usually the first square bears the maker's initials.

Just to add variety, some craftsmen, like David Melvil of Newport, Rhode Island (1755-1793), impressed some of their pieces with two different marks, both their own. In general, simple name touches, like "R. Dunham," in an oblong frame, are those of men who worked in the "coffeepot" era. Another group of American pewter sometimes seen in dealer's shops is that with two marks, neither of them that of a known maker.

I have owned a plate for at least twenty-five years that has a rose and crown device not too distinctly impressed, and as its other mark the word "LQNDON" in what printers call "all capitals, bold face." I have seen others like it in dealers' shops. Nobody is certain what these plates are. I am inclined to class them as done by American craftsmen who practiced a little chicanery when they marked them. As I see it, they purposely omitted their own mark and used the rose and crown or other device characteristic of a number of English pewterers, together with the word LONDON slightly misspelled to give the impression that pewter so marked was of the superior imported kind rather than a home product. Preference for things imported from England as against those of domestic make is no new thing, and if my deductions are correct, this pewter plate proves that our native craftsmen sometimes used a trick or two to cope with this preference.

A large amount of nineteenth-century English pewter, sold in the United States for some years before 1850, bore the mark of Dixon of Birmingham, who did fine work and produced a large number of tea and coffee services, which were in much demand for the American market. English-made pewter of this type was the chief competitor of that made by our American pewterers.

Most English pewter was marked, and this was controlled by the London Company of Pewterers or its provincial equivalent in such important pewter-making towns as Bristol, Exeter, York or Birmingham. There was, however, a considerable quantity by country pewterers which was never marked at all. Much of the pewter imported by colonial Americans is now thought to have been this unmarked kind. In fact, marking of pewter was not as standardized in England as was that of silver, probably because of pewter's lesser value. Most common of the English pewter marks is a large device of rose and crown, with the maker's name or initials lettered in the border. Also, there frequently are a series of small punches that look like hallmarks on silver but do not include a date letter.

Nearly six hundred craftsmen who made pewter in England between 1700 and 1847 are known, and their marks are given in *Old Pewter, Its Makers and Marks in England, Scotland and Ireland,* by Howard Herschel Cotterell. Most of the English pewter available to collectors is of later eighteenth- or early nineteenth-century production. Earlier pieces are very rare, although items dating back to 1500 or before are found occasionally.

Pewter made in France, Germany, Holland, Switzerland and other Continental countries also bears makers' marks. Study of them is a specialty of its own. Books on such pewter can be found in reference libraries of the larger museums, but are usually in French or German. The only one in English is *National Types of Old Pewter,* also written by Mr. Cotterell, who has made a study of ways to determine the nationality of foreign pewter by form and pattern.

There is one kind of pewter, American or European, that the collector should leave alone. It is antique and genuine, but diseased. It is called "sick pewter" and some collectors will not have a piece so affected anywhere near their other pewter, because of fear of contamination. This fear, I think, is not based on fact, since pewter, being inorganic, is not subject to contagion. Just what are the causes of sick pewter is not known, but the result is obvious to anyone who has tried to remedy such a piece. Somehow, by corrosion or otherwise, oxidation of the alloy is not just on the surface; it has penetrated so deeply that it cannot be removed. Treat it with acid or lye long enough to remove all oxidation, and there is no pewter left. This condition may be likened to an incurable metallic cancer.

I have seen both collectors and dealers try all their secret tricks on pieces of this sort with never a successful result. I have been told also that efforts to melt sick pewter and cast spoons of it will not work. So the best advice I can give is never knowingly to buy a piece where oxidation has gone that far. But if, unwittingly, you should acquire such a piece, do not waste time or material trying to effect a cure. No matter how hard you work, a dull, leadlike gray color persists. You never attain a surface that can be polished, and sometimes the piece falls apart in your hands as you work on it.

Brass and copper are closely related metals from which useful and highly decorative accessories were made as household gear. Those of brass, in addition to furniture hardware already commented upon, were chiefly related to heating and lighting the home. There were the brass andirons and fenders, the fireplace tools with their decorative brass handles, the warming pans with which the chill of beds in those ill-heated early homes was remedied, and a considerable assortment of candlesticks. There were also open kettles, coated with block tin on the inside and equipped with swinging bails of wrought iron, which were used for cooking in the big open fireplaces.

Of these brasses, andirons and candlesticks appeal most to collectors. In only a few instances are andirons found with matching sets of fireplace tools (tongs, shovel and poker). Even rarer are those with a matching brass fender.

Practically all antique American brass andirons available today date after 1785. Rare and desirable are those made between that date and 1820. Desirable but more numerous are examples produced between 1820 and 1840 or 1850. It was during this latter period that most andirons of the knobby baluster design were made. Designs of those made earlier were classic columns, a series of spheres in graduated sizes, large spheres surmounting baluster-shaped columns, and spherical shapes terminating in steeple finials.

Among the rare marked examples are andirons by Paul Revere, which date after he turned from silversmithing to casting bells and cannon. They are generally marked "P. Revere and Sons." John Molyneaux and a brass founder named David, both of Boston, made and marked steeple-top andirons. Also Henry Noyes of Bangor, Maine, marked his distinctive andirons of the low ball-finial design, and Richard Whittingham of New York produced very fine large andirons of classic column design with urn-shaped finials. His incised mark read "R.Whittingham N.York."

Antique brass andirons can be quickly identified if one knows what to look for, and where. First, the hollow decorative front posts were cast in halves and then put together by braising before being turned smooth on a lathe. If one will breath on the polished brass posts, two silver-like lines can be seen on opposite sides. Some have maintained that these brass halves were put together with a silver solder, but this interesting conjecture is not borne out by fact. The braising compound consisted of brass filings mixed with a fluxing agent, such as borax. Braising was done at a high heat, during which more of the copper than of the zinc was consumed—hence the silver color that marks the braised joints.

If the andirons are so tarnished that the "silver hair line" cannot be seen, unscrew one of the uprights. By looking at the rough interior you can see where the two parts were joined. Second, you will note that the threads of the wrought-iron vertical rod that hold these brass parts in position are hand-cut with a file, and that the rods themselves still bear the irregular sledge marks of their hand-forging on a blacksmith's anvil.

This same test can be used to identify andirons of a later date. Here the interior surface will be smooth. The iron rod also is smooth and has a machine-cut thread, and the tip of the brass finial is a separate part forming a small nut that, when tightened, holds the sections beneath firm. Andirons so constructed date from about 1870, when brass spinning of circular shapes had replaced "half-casting." With such andirons, machinemade iron rods about three-eighths of an inch in diameter were fastened to the legs by machine-cut bolts instead of being hammered fast when red-hot.

Even later are brass andirons of the so-called Russian brass-shop period. These date after 1910. Workmanship of the brass parts is crude and sloppy; the horizontals on which the wood rests are generally of cast iron, instead of the stronger and more durable wrought iron. Such andirons were made largely by immigrants who had fled Russia because of the wide-spread pogroms which were part of the general unrest in that country after the Russian-Japanese War.

Fireplace tools with cast-brass handles are judged by their iron parts. The arms of tongs, shaft and shovel blades, and poker rods were hand-forged. Consequently, marks of hammer blows and a certain roughness can be observed. Less desirable, though very well made, are those fireplace tools produced between 1860 and 1890 of machine-made iron stock. Smoothness of parts dates them, but the handcraft aim of making things that would last has carried over sufficiently so that they are not out of place among other antiques. Not as much can be said of modern fireplace tools.

Along with brass andirons, some American-made pairs are found with a definite reddish color. These are of bell metal, a slightly different alloy than brass, which was compounded of seventy parts of copper to thirty of zinc. Bell metal was composed of eighty parts copper to twenty of tin. This difference in formula and the larger proportion of copper accounts for the reddish tone.

Candlesticks of brass and sometimes of bell metal were, as early as the middle of the seventeenth century, part of the household equipment of American families who could afford them. Practically all of those used during our colonial period were imported from England. Brass founding was discouraged on this side of the Atlantic in an effort to make as much business as possible for the workers of Birmingham, England. These colonial candlesticks varied somewhat, but in general they were baluster-shaped, with ample bases and large saucer-like elements beneath the candleholders to catch the wax drippings. Sticks of this sort are rare indeed today and are seldom seen outside of museums or extensive private collections.

Most of the candlesticks found in antique shops are of early nineteenth-century production. Usually they are modified baluster shapes, with square or octagon bases. They are of fairly thin cast metal, turned smooth on lathes, but with the interior retaining the roughness of sand casting. Inserted in the hollow interior of such a stick is a slender iron rod with button-like ends. This was used to eject the stub end of a candle from its socket. Sometimes this ejector arrangement is broken or missing. Such candlesticks, though not as desirable as those which are complete, should not be rejected because of this.

Other antique candlesticks, chiefly for bedroom use, were made of sheet brass, with ample dishlike bases and curved handles. They were in square and circular shapes. Large ones are often used today for ash trays. Old sticks of this sort were of thicker sheet metal, and their ringlike handles were riveted to the dish-shaped bases on the underside. They should not be confused with another type of bedroom candlestick, usually smaller sized, which was made of cast brass about 1880, or with still later ones of light-gauge sheet metal, made after 1910 and sold when new by art and gift shops.

The Russian brass shops, which were originally located along Allen Street in the heart of New York's East Side, have made and sold a quantity of brass candlesticks and candelabras, but in designs that never more than approximate the antique and are often totally different. Most of them are solid metal, and where one part screws into another the threads are machine-cut. Also made in these shops were seven-branch candlesticks, originally intended for religious use in Jewish households. Today they are found far afield, as are the cast-brass candlesticks with saucer base and with a small bell hung in a yoke beneath the candle socket. These are modern, and so different in appearance from antique candlesticks that only the most unobservant would confuse them.

Antique brass open kettles, used for fireplace cooking, were beaten from sheet metal, had a heavy rolled rim and two brackets riveted on the outside to which a wrought-iron semi-circular bail was attached, and the interiors were coated with block tin to keep the brass from discoloring food cooked in them. Usually some of the hammer marks can still be seen, showing how such kettles were beaten and shaped. Occasionally one sees a warming pan of brass or copper, with long handle of wood or wrought iron, though such pieces are mostly not found outside museums, because some twenty or thirty years ago there was a vogue for converting the lids into sconcelike electric-lighting fixtures. Consequently, warming pans in undamaged condition are scarce.

Teakettles and various sizes of open kettles were apt to be made of copper. Old teakettles can be readily recognized by the dovetail joints that show where the sheet of metal was lapped on the sides and where the bottom was joined to the sides. The graceful curve of the spout, often swanlike and materially larger where it was soldered to the kettle than at the pouring end, is another characteristic of one of these squat, bulbous copper teakettles. Some were made with wrought-iron handles; others with a flat strip of copper curved into a decorative shape; and still others with hollow copper handles, either with or without a nicely ring-turned wooden center.

Those of American origin should not be confused with the more elaborately shaped ones of European or Near East provenance. Although the latter range from simple cylinders to squat, bulbous bodies with long upward flaring necks, all are so unlike the teakettles of American make or those produced in England and exported here when new that the collector should find it easy to distinguish them.

Copper teakettles made watertight by a folded seam instead of by a dovetailed or braised one are not old enough to rank as antiques, although they may look worn. They were only partially handmade and date from about 1875, or the beginning of factory production of such utensils. This is particularly true of teakettles in which the rim of the bottom is pinched onto the lower edge of the sides.

In addition to preserving kettles of from two quarts to five gallons, a wide variety of basins, pans and muglike measures were also made of copper. The antique ones can usually be recognized by their dovetailed or braised seams, simple handles, either of copper or iron, and their utilitarian shapes. Today these antique receptacles are used by collectors as fruit bowls and flower containers.

CHAPTER VIII

Prints of Varied Types and Kinds

As wall decorations, nothing complements antique furniture more effectively than old prints. Their wide range of subjects offer the collector a variety to choose from and they blend with practically all the old style periods.

For instance, I once saw a dining room furnished with American Chippendale furniture, including display cupboards filled with Oriental Lowestoft, where the chief wall decoration was a large folio Currier & Ives print of Eastman Johnson's painting "Husking." This colorful farm scene with the figures in plain working clothes hung above the mantel. The claw and ball-footed table and chairs antedated the print by at least ninety years and were sophisticated pieces of urban craftsmanship. Yet there was no clash, but rather a pleasing contrast.

Another example was a guest room furnished in maple, which included a Queen Anne highboy, a Hepplewhite bow-front chest of drawers, a Sheraton tripod bedside table and Empire fiddle-back chairs. Here a pleasing touch was added by three English prints (two from Thornton's *Temple of Flora,* done in 1812, and a Gould bird print) and a map of the locality from a typical county atlas published about 1860. A guest doubtless found these much more restful than the assortment of family and school group photographs that are sometimes hung in such "spare rooms" for want of a better place.

American prints are most favored by collectors. Subject groupings include portraits of prominent people, from presidents to prize fighters; outstanding events, from naval engagements to conflagrations; localities, city views or country scenes; genre depictions of social customs that have passed; prints that are records of the economic development of the United States, such as clipper ships, early railroads and volunteer fire companies; sports, such as horse racing, hunting and fishing, yachting and the start of baseball; early views of American colleges; and comic and sentimental prints. In point of age, these prints range from the Burgis view of Harvard, done in 1726, to a lithograph of the Brooklyn Bridge, published as late as 1890 by Currier & Ives.

There are three main kinds of prints—engravings, lithographs and woodcuts. Engravings were executed by artists or by technically skilled craftsmen who copied their pictures on metal plates, from which the printing was done. With plates of copper, five distinct types of prints could be executed. They were line engravings, mezzotints, etchings, stipples and aquatints. Line engraving was printed with black ink and coloring was added afterward by hand. Etchings were also done with black ink. Some mezzotints were colored after they came from the press; for others, two or more colors of ink were used in printing. Coloring was part of the process with stipple engravings and aquatints.

Prints from copper-plate engravings mostly date before 1840. From about 1850 to 1875 a quantity of steel engravings were published. They included such subjects as "Marriage of Pocohontas," "The Death Bed of Daniel Webster," and "The Pilgrims Going to Church." They lack the quality of the earlier copper-plate engravings and because of their size (24 by 36 inches or larger) are not popular with collectors. They are classed as late and do not command nearly as high prices as contemporary Currier & Ives lithographs. Their appeal is limited to collectors particularly interested in the subjects depicted.

Lithographs were printed from stones on which the pictures were drawn in outline by the artists or by draftsmen working for the publishers. After the printing in black and white, they were hand-colored by young women working in teams, somewhat like a modern factory assembly line. American lithographs date from 1835 to as late as 1900. They were usually published in three sizes—large folio, 17 by 24 inches; medium folio, 11 by 15 inches; and small folio, 8 by 12 inches.

N. Currier, starting in 1835, and Currier & Ives from 1857, were the great publishers of such prints. Any lithograph bearing either of these imprints is collectible, and some are rarities. "The Life of a Hunter—a Tight Fix," by Currier & Ives, holds the record for the highest price paid at an auction. In 1928 this print brought $3,000. The price has not been equaled since then.

About 1865, a form of lithographic printing that eliminated hand-coloring was introduced, known as chromolithography. Some interesting prints were produced by this method, but they are considered late, are not much in demand and usually sell at fairly low prices. Louis Prang of Boston was the most important publisher of them.

Woodcuts were printed from blocks of wood on which the artists or special craftsmen cut the pictures. Most of these prints were of a size suitable for book or magazine illustrations. The majority date from about 1850, with a few very early ones going back to the colonial period. As important an American artist as Winslow Homer made a good many drawings as an artist war correspondent during the War between The States, which were published as woodcuts in *Harper's Weekly*. They are collectible and inexpensive. Many woodcuts of buildings, localities and important events are removed from old books or magazines, nicely hand-tinted and framed. These are often the only pictorial records available and are desirable for such reasons. I have one in my collection, of "Lana Cascade," Lake Dunmore, Salisbury, Vermont, which is the only print of this waterfall. As the waterfall no longer exists, this woodcut is doubly interesting.

The majority of American prints found in antique shops are lithographs published by Currier & Ives and their many contemporaries. A few of the better known were Pendleton, in whose Boston shop Nathaniel Currier worked as an apprentice, Bufford, Kellogg, Baillie, Endicott, Rosenthal, Sarony, Knapp & Major, and Britton & Rey of San Francisco. These lithographs range in price from a few dollars for sentimental subjects done as small folio prints to sums in three or four figures for large folio rarities.

Condition should always be taken into consideration in buying such a print. Blemishes such as tears, creases, stains and cut margins, even though slight, reduce its value. To rate as in prime condition, a print should be free of the brownish stains known as "foxing," should have its full margins, be free of creases in the paper, and not be torn along the outer edges. The latter defect is sometimes skillfully repaired, and if it does not extend into the actual picture is not too detrimental. Coloring should also be clear and unfaded.

As stated earlier, originally all lithographs came from the press as black and white outline impressions and were then hand-colored. Since some uncolored copies were sold to art teachers, examples of these "albino" prints are occasionally found today. Sometimes, particularly with the more desirable subjects, this lack of color is rectified by colorists using full colored originals as their guide. This late work can usually be recognized by the brilliance of the individual colors. A print that has been recently colored will not be offered to a prospective buyer by a print dealer of good repute without stating what has been done and the price asked will be less than if the coloring were contemporary with the printing.

Some full-size copies have also been brought out of such popular prints as "Home to Thanksgiving." These are not done as fakes but as acknowledged re-issues. Here careful reading of the fine lettering immediately below the picture

THE FAMOUS "HOME TO THANKSGIVING" PRINT

This was lithographed by Currier & Ives from a painting by Charles Durrie. Winter scene prints from his originals, all published by Currier & Ives, have long ranked high with collectors.

A FEDERAL HALL PRINT

This view of the first Capitol of the United States was engraved in 1789 by S. Hull as an illustration for the Massachusetts Magazine. Amos Doolittle made a similar engraving showing Washington taking his oath of office as our first president.

ABOVE: This early 18th century settle was painted with several coats. These coats should be removed, the piece thoroughly sandpapered, then done over with three coats of shellac or paint.

BELOW—LEFT: Vermont armchair of about 1820. Rockers were removed, legs lengthened, new finials applied to front uprights, with other touches. CENTER: A New Hampshire chair about 1800. It was reseated with rush and the frame given three coats 25 years ago. Note shortening of legs, indicating a previous conversion to desk chair. RIGHT: Armchair, Connecticut, ca. 1775. Has not been repaired. Two inches taken off legs 100 years ago in order to mount it as a wheel chair.

This New England Queen Anne tea table was found covered by several coats of paint. When removed it was a combination of maple legs and cherry top and arched skirts but was entirely original.

REFINISHED BY AN EXPERT

This American serpentine-front chest of drawers was carefully refinished to preserve the rich tone of the mahogany. This would have been lost too thorough scraping had taken place. The brasses are excellent replacements.

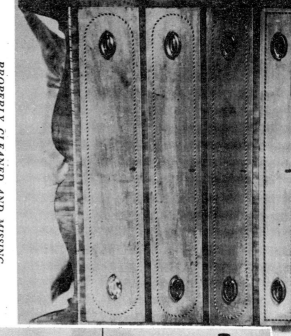

PROPERLY CLEANED AND MISSING INLAY REPLACED

This *American Hepplewhite* chest of drawers was photographed after the old finish had been removed, some small pieces of inlay replaced and the whole piece thoroughly smoothed with fine sandpaper, but before it was refinished. The oval brasses are the original ones.

CHAIR CLEANED TO THE WOOD

This shows how any chair will look when the old coats of paint have been removed. The four turned feet are missing and should be replaced. Also cracks in the arm should be filled with plastic wood before the frame is refinished. It should also be provided with a new rush seat woven over the upper stretches. If done tightly it will make the chair much firmer.

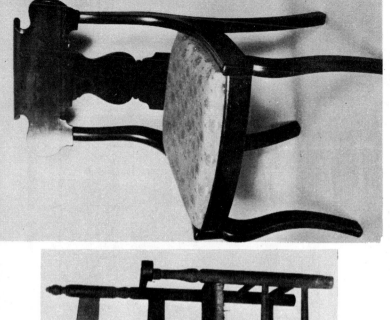

*LEFT: ORIGINAL WAGON
SEAT REFINISHED*

Five coats of paint were removed by gasoline torch, so
carefully that turnings of
finials and rush of old seat
were not scorched. Frame
was refinished with three
coats of green-black paint,
sandpapered after each coat.
Uncomfortable tilt of back
was corrected by "domes of
silence" applied to front legs.
Made in Westchester Coun-
ty, N. Y., about 1800. Originally one of a set of three.

RIGHT: A COMPLETE WRECK

It had been put out for the garbage man. Top cross member was broken where it was attached to
back legs which were also split at seat level. That was repaired by gluing; then frame was
scraped and refinished.

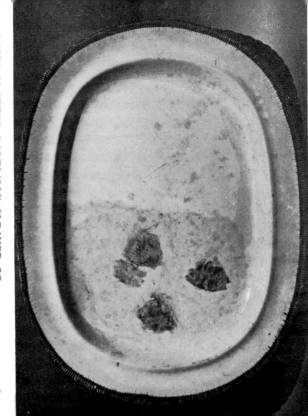

LEEDS PLATTER PARTIALLY CLEANED OF FOOD AND AGE STAINS

The left half was coated with paraffin; the platter was then filled with Clorox and allowed to soak for several days. The two halves demonstrate how brownish stains beneath the glaze may be removed or materially lessened. Both porcelains and earthenware respond to this treatment.

RIVETS USED IN CHINA REPAIR

Repairmen can put broken pieces together or stop cracks from spreading by the use of one-inch double-pointed rivets of iron wire. These are seated by drilling small parallel holes into the ware into which the points of the rivets are driven by sharp blows. Further spread of two aged cracks was checked nearly fifty years ago in this 13 inch Staffordshire blue and white transfer ware bowl by inserting ten rivets.

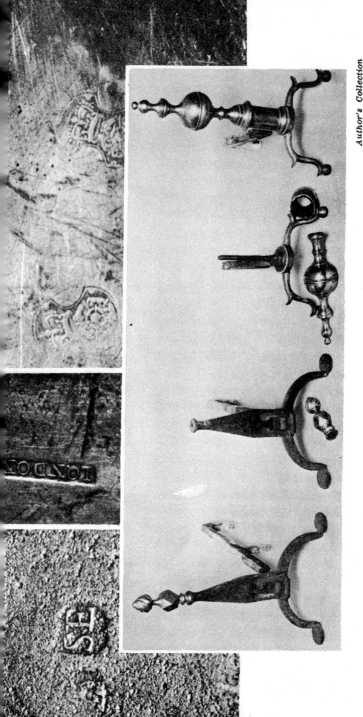

Pewter touch marks in the background. At left the initials SE are the mark of Simon Edgell, Philadelphia 1713-1742. At right note the two rose and crown marks, and LONDON spelled LQNDON. Probably late 18th century English provincial or American attempting to be English.

In the foreground are antique and later andirons. The brass pair at right date about 1825. Front column of one has been unscrewed to show antique method of half-casting and the hand-filed screw of the supporting iron rod. The iron pair at left are obvious copies—shown by hammer marks and shape of uprights and machine-cut screws at base of brass finials. Probably made from originals 25 years ago.

GOOD, POOR AND BAD PEWTER

Large plate at left shows an average pewter plate in good enough condition to polish easily. The fine scratches are knife cuts. A spot where a hole was repaired with solder can be seen in rim at top. The center plate is badly pitted. In cleaning, it was boiled with a lye solution, then buffed on a fine-wire wheel. Oxidation and corrosion went so deep as to leave pit marks that mar the piece and materially reduce its value. At right we have a plate of sick pewter. Here deterioration has gone too far to yield to any cleaning method. Pieces like this are considered valueless by collectors.

will identify such a print for what it is—an honest copy made much later than the time of the original.

These do not rate as "restrikes," which were subsequent re-issues done from the same copper plates or lithographic stones used when the print was first published. These re-strikes bear much the same relation to prints as subsequent editions of a book do to the first edition, except that later book printings bear on the title page the dates when they were done. Except in rare instances, re-strikes carry nothing in the caption data to distinguish them from earlier impressions. They can usually be identified by inferiority of the paper on which they are printed. It is lighter in weight and has a harder surface.

In the 1930's, some of the most popular of the Currier & Ives prints were reprinted in quantity and widely sold in five-and-ten-cent stores. They were all smaller in size than the originals. Coloring was part of the press work, and the paper was not of the same thickness or texture as in the originals. Of about the same vintage are the pictures copied from some of the Currier & Ives prints and used on large calendars issued for several years by a large insurance company. Some of these were trimmed and mounted by people who admired them and are now occasionally offered to collectors by uninformed people as Currier & Ives prints. These calendar copies are much smaller than the large folio originals. The coloring is an integral part of the press work and the paper is much smoother and thinner than was ever used by Currier & Ives. They also lack proper margins, especially at the bottom.

For further information regarding Currier & Ives prints, the standard book is *Currier & Ives, Printmakers to the American People,* by Harry T. Peters. Equally authoritative is the author's other work, *America on Stone,* which includes the other American lithographers and the prints they published. We might mention here, for those interested in pictorial sheet-music covers, which are among the collectibles, that *Early American Sheet Music,* by Harry Dichter and Elliott Shapiro, is a book worth consulting.

Prints done from copper-plate engravings offer the collector a wide choice. Those made during the eighteenth century were mostly scenic or historic as to subject and are now expensive rarities. Among them are the Harvard College print already mentioned, that of the Boston Massacre by Paul Revere, and the fine mezzotint portrait of Sir William Pepperell. This was the work of Peter Pelham, an English artist who settled in Boston, where he married the Widow Copley and became the stepfather of John Singleton Copley, the greatest native American painter of the colonial period.

Following the American Revolution and continuing until about 1830, many prints depicting historic events, scenic views and prominent people were published, which are now highly desirable rarities. Among the men who were both artists and engravers was Amos Doolittle of New Haven, Connecticut, probably best known for his print of the Federal Hall in New York City, which depicted Washington taking his oath of office as the first president of the United States. Another was Charles D.J.F. de St. Memin, the French refugee whose small profile portrait prints of prominent patriots are rarities. Still others were William H. Bartlett, who did the *American Scenery* series; William R. Birch, known especially for his Philadelphia views; Samuel Maverick, a New York engraver who drew and engraved the print of the "Landing of Lafayette," which was reproduced by Clewes, a Staffordshire potter, on his blue and white china; and William G.Wall, famous for his *Hudson River Portfolio.*

Any engraved print of an American subject of this period is a desirable collectible, as are others down to the time of the large steel engraving vogue. Some of the men who did them had colorful careers, like the counterfeiter, Christian Meadows, who engraved a print of Dartmouth College, now much sought for, while serving a prison sentence for his sins against the law.

Along with American prints, many collectors are partial to the wide range of English prints, among them caricatures by Thomas Rowlandson that are frequently quite broad in their treatment. There are also very fine flower prints, such as Thornton's *Temple of Flora* and the beautiful bird prints by Gould. Also in England, between 1827 and 1838, Havell executed the elephant folio aquatints for Audobon's *Birds of America*. Prints from this, especially the "Wild Turkey," are very high-priced. Less expensive, but by no means cheap, are the same subjects from the American edition of 1860 of this work and those from Audubon's other great accomplishment, *The Quadrupeds of North America,* published in New York in 1845 and 1846 with a hundred and fifty colored lithographic plates.

There have been a number of books on various phases of prints, but the best general volume is *The Quest of the Print,* by Frank Weitenkampf, who was special librarian of the print collection of the New York Public Library for over twenty years. Also an excellent collection of American town and city views of the nineteenth century is on permanent display in the main building of this library, on Fifth Avenue at 42nd Street. These prints are hung along the corridors of the general reading room floor and each is labeled as to subject and date.

PART TWO

CHAPTER IX

Refinishing Antique Furniture

It is well known that many collectors seized with the urge to do their own work start with refinishing and gradually progress to repair work. To the beginner, refinishing looks easy—anyone could do it. Just keep applying remover until the old finish has disappeared, rub a little with sandpaper and put on a coat or two of varnish or shellac. But anyone who tries it usually has his doubts about its being "easy" long before the process of removing the old finish has been completed. If he flounders on and sees the work through, according to his preconceived ideas, the result is likely to be a botched job or a ruined piece.

The collector who wants to do right by his antique furniture should remember that a little goes a long way. The nearer a piece can be kept to its original condition, the better. A complete job, starting with remover, should only be undertaken if the old finish has been worn away, badly damaged or buried beneath subsequent coats of paint or varnish. Then, and only then, is it necessary to get back to the wood and build up a new protective coating.

Granted that much antique furniture is found in such rough condition that complete refinishing is obviously necessary, yet there are pieces where the original finish can be preserved. This is true of mahogany, walnut, maple or cherry antiques with the old varnish finish. It also holds with a considerable group of country-made pieces where the original finish was New England red filler or the distinctive off-shade known as "Amish blue." Even painted furniture, including Windsor chairs, done in various colors or in a brownish shade over which a crude graining was applied, sometimes has enough of its original finish so that restoration rather than refinishing is the answer.

Therefore, study your piece well before operating. If there is a chance of preserving the original finish, take it, and know that you are salvaging a valued indication of genuineness. Moreover, although preserving the original finish takes plenty of time and patience, it does not entail anywhere near as much hard work as removing it and building up the new finish. I know, for I have done both.

At this point, I would suggest to anyone who has never tried restoring or refinishing a piece of furniture that he begin with a simple piece, such as a light stand with tapered legs or a chest of drawers without carving, reeding or inlay. Such pieces are relatively inexpensive and it is better for a beginner to try his hand on such a piece, because the work will be easier and if the results are not all that might be desired, something rare and fine has not been sacrificed. I know of no royal road to the mastery of refinishing furniture. It has to be gained by trial and error.

With a piece that looks as if its original varnish finish might be retained, the first step is to clean it thoroughly. This gets rid of the accumulated dirt and grease that sometimes form such a thick coating as to make it hard to determine whether the wood is mahogany, cherry or the "red" Virginia walnut used by eighteenth-century cabinetmakers. It can also hide the fine lines of inlay. Incidentally, this greasy film is not usually so much the result of bad housekeeping as of repeated polishings with low-grade furniture cosmetics, such as the so-called lemon oil, sold in dime stores. These polishes contain little else than a light oil derived from petroleum and a small percentage of paraffin. These, being mineral products, are never absorbed, but remain on the surface catching dust until the piece eventually achieves a true pancake make-up.

For this cleaning I prefer carbon tetrachloride. It can be bought in gallon containers at most paint stores. I find it dissolves dirt and grease readily, does not soften either varnish or shellac and, being non-inflammable, is safe. Benzine or gasoline that is free of the "anti-knock" compound can also be used, but because of the fire hazard, do this washing out of doors and do not bring the piece indoors for several hours, or until you are sure that all the liquid has evaporated. Less expensive than either is plain soap and water, though it should be used carefully; otherwise it may prove to be a case of "penny wise, pound foolish."

Since water will loosen any glued joint, and also tends to raise the grain of the wood, don't attack the piece as though you were washing Fido. Give it a sponge bath, using as little water as possible and wringing the cloth nearly dry. Never use even that on veneered or inlaid furniture. No matter how carefully done, some of the water is bound to soak through and moisten the glue beneath. It may not be noticeable at the time, but a little later places on the veneered surface begin to bulge or come loose and small pieces of inlay will raise up just enough to catch and break. Regluing loose veneer and replacing missing inlay is delicate work; amateurs should not attempt it.

In washing a piece with either carbon tetrachloride or benzine, use a small stiff-bristled scrub brush on any places where the caked-on dirt and grease cling stubbornly. One of the dry-cleaning compounds, soluble in either of these liquids, is helpful but should be used sparingly. Whichever cleaning agent is used, work carefully and do a little at a time, especially until you get the hang of it. Make an initial try of a small area that does not show, such as the under side of a table top between the edge and the bed. Its finish will be the same as the rest of the piece and by experimenting there you will know better how to proceed in cleaning the rest of the surface.

After you have finished cleaning the piece, rinse with fresh liquid, wipe with clean rags and set it aside to dry for twenty-four hours. You will be surprised at how much of the old finish was concealed under the dirt and grime.

Now, in a good light, examine your piece carefully. There may be some small spots or minor areas where the old finish is gone or is badly worn, but if most of it is intact, even though dull and somewhat scratched, it can be brought back with nothing more mysterious than raw linseed oil, turpentine and beeswax. Plenty of time, patience and hard rubbing will be needed, but faithful observation of all three will result in a nicely polished piece of furniture with original finish. This speaks more effectively of genuineness than the best refinishing ever can.

The next step is what museum curators refer to as "feeding." This can take several weeks, with long waits in between. By it, the old varnish and wood fibers beneath, which have become dried out through the years, are renewed. Place the piece where it will not have to be moved and where no dust will blow on it. Then, using a clean paint brush from an inch to two inches wide, coat it with the best grade of raw linseed oil you can obtain. But don't overdo it. Just stroke on an even coat that completely covers the surfaces but doesn't stand in pools. The place selected for the piece undergoing this treatment should remain at room temperature (68 to 70 degrees) or more, for linseed oil becomes stiff and thick if it gets cold. A place by a sunny window is ideal, as the warmth of the sun helps the oil to penetrate. I know of one man who puts such pieces in a disused flower conservatory. He finds the sunlight materially speeds absorption and improves results.

The linseed oil for this first coat and others that follow may be warmed in a double boiler for better penetration. Wear a pair of leather work gloves, for a spatter of hot oil can cause a bad burn. Stay right with the brew as it heats,

for it catches fire easily. Test it several times by dipping the
tip of a brush in the oil. It should never be allowed to boil
or become hot enough to scorch the brush bristles.

When you have finished giving the piece its initial coat,
rebottle and cork the linseed oil and clean the brush thoroughly with turpentine so that the oil will not thicken or the
brush become gummy between times. Let the piece stand for
several days to a week, until as much of the oil as possible
has been absorbed. Then wipe the piece thoroughly with
clean soft cloths to remove any excess, which by then will
have become slightly sticky. Repaint with a fresh coat of oil.
This may have to be done three, four, or even five times with
the same periods of rest between. The successive coats will
be absorbed more and more slowly. Stop the oil treatment
when the last coat does not seem to be absorbed to any extent
after it has stood for at least a week. Wipe the piece thoroughly until no trace of oil can be found on the cloth.

During the resting intervals, some underside spot can be
tested to discover whether the original finish was varnish or
shellac. For this test, saturate a small piece of blotting paper
with alcohol. Place it on the test spot and let it remain there
for a few minutes. If the finish was shellac, the alcohol will
have softened it and some will adhere to the paper; if varnish,
the alcohol will have no effect. With this information, you
know what to use in touching up any spots, small worn places
or pronounced scratches. Ordinary series of fine scratches are
not noticeable enough to be considered, and will be taken
care of in the final polishing.

With an old varnish finish, touch up the worn places
with a fine grade of new. That known as violin maker's varnish is expensive but produces the best results. Thin it to
about the consistency of pancake sirup and apply lightly with
a small badger-hair brush to the places where the old finish is
missing. A day or so later, when such spotting is thoroughly
dry, remove any brush marks from the new varnish and dull

it slightly with the finest grade of powdered emery or pumice stone. A good method is to use the tip of a finger or a small cork, first moistened with very light lubricating oil and then lightly dusted with the abrasive. Work very gently, for the purpose is to remove brush marks and "kill" the high gloss of the patching varnish. Such touching may have to be repeated once or twice until spots so treated are not noticeable.

If the test has shown that the original finish was shellac, use either orange or white shellac for spotting, depending on whether the surrounding surface is very clear or has a slight nut-brown cast. Cut the shellac with about a quarter as much alcohol, and apply it deftly with a small hair brush. Two or three coats will be necessary, and each one when thoroughly dry should be smoothed slightly with 0000 sandpaper to remove brush marks and surface gloss, just as with varnish spotting.

The final step is polishing the entire piece. There are a number of good prepared waxes that can be bought in paint and hardware stores, but I prefer to make my own, using beeswax and turpentine. I consider it better and know it is less expensive. A quart of it will polish a good many pieces of furniture. Shave a pound cake of beeswax in fine pieces with a heavy knife or wide chisel. Put it in a wide-mouthed glass jar or kitchen bowl. Add about half as much turpentine; cover and place in a sunny spot until the warmth has melted the wax. Then if it is stiffer than average heavy automobile engine oil, add more turpentine, a little at a time, and stir thoroughly to get an even consistency.

With the mixture still warm and liquid, apply very lightly. Let the piece stand in a cool but not cold place, out of direct sunlight, for a day or more until the wax is almost hard. Then, with pieces of light stiff cardboard (I use discarded playing cards), remove as much wax as possible and return it to the jar to be stirred into the mixture and used again. Follow by quite vigorous but not heavy-handed rubbing with clean cloths until no trace of the wax comes off on the cloth.

For this polishing, nothing is better than a piece of white flannel or part of an old light-weight woolen blanket. Whether cotton, linen or woolen cloths are used, be sure that they are free from dust. Fine gritty particles are apt to leave scratches that mar the finish. For a satin-smooth polish, use relatively little wax and plenty of elbow grease. There are circular fabric polishing attachments on the market designed for use with small electric portable drills. If handled carefully, one of these can shorten the time required to get a proper polish. But if too much pressure is used, such a device will do more harm than good, so I prefer the all-hand method, even though it takes longer and is harder work.

Waxing may have to be repeated a second or even a third time to achieve a truly fine polish, but once a piece is finished, a light polishing once or twice a year will keep it in first-rate condition. Also, if water or other liquid is spilled on a surface so treated, such as a table top, the fine film of wax protects it from damage and telltale white spots. As far as I know, there are no short cuts or time savers that can be employed, except the dubious one of a power-driven polishing tool already mentioned. The work is slow and at times distinctly tedious, but the results are worth it.

The all-hand method is the one followed by the large museums in preparing a new acquisition for display. Such a piece may remain in the museum's furniture workshop for months. Sometimes the technicians find that although it has been revarnished several times in the course of years, the original finish underneath is intact. Then, working almost in the manner of a painting restorer and taking a very small space at a time, later layers of varnish are lifted off with bits of absorbent cotton moistened in solvent. After this has been accomplished, the process of oil "feeding" is begun. It is because of such extreme care that many of the pieces in large museum collections look almost as fresh as the day they were delivered to their original owners by the craftsmen who made them. Close to a year was required by one of our best-known museums to clean a matching Philadelphia highboy and lowboy and bring back the matchless bloom of their original finish.

For a piece on which original painted finish is to be restored, the process is the same as with a varnish or shellac finish, except that the spotting is, of course, done with paint, carefully mixed to match the original.

With antique furniture, where the finish is beyond hope, which is frequently the case with tables that were relegated to the kitchen or were "modernized" at various times with one or more coats of paint, the only course of action is to strip off what is left of the old finish or later paint.

Start by making a test at some inconspicuous place so that you may know what the conditions are. What is the wood? Is it a veneered piece? Is it decorated with inlay? It is important to know as much as possible about the conditions that face you. Then adapt your methods to meet them. For instance, if it is an early tavern table with pine top, a steel scraper should be used very sparingly. It is too apt to bite into such soft wood and destroy the time-mellowed patina of the surface. If it is a veneered or inlaid piece, using one of the home-concocted remover solutions of lye, soap powder, ammonia and water would be fatal. If the piece is of curly or birds-eye maple or other fancy-grained wood, there is hard work ahead in removing the old finish from such irregular texture. If the piece was originally covered with the red paintlike mixture known as New England filler, removing all traces of it will be a big undertaking. It was put on boiling hot, and consequently struck deep into the pores of the wood. Sometimes, with coarser grained woods, it penetrated as much as a sixteenth of an inch. Under such conditions, it is better to refinish with a paint that approximates the tone of the old New

England red rather than to try to "bring it up" in natural wood color.*

For removing old finish, two methods are available. That usually followed is to use one of the prepared removers that can be bought at paint or hardware stores. All contain fairly quick-acting substances that soften paint or varnish so that it can be wiped off with cloths or scraped off with a putty knife or steel scraper. If the piece, as too often happens, has several layers of varnish or paint, or a combination of both, you may have to brush on the liquid remover several times. In using any remover, read the directions on the can and follow them closely. Most of them are inflammable, so do not smoke as you work. Also, since most removers evaporate quickly and give off fumes that can make the eyes smart or bring on a headache, don't work without plenty of fresh air. Have at least one window open, or better still, do the work out of doors. As a further precaution, protect the eyes with driving goggles against a chance spatter, and wear rubber gloves and a work shirt with long sleeves, since some removers can cause an uncomfortable burn. It is also a good idea to have a can of benzine at hand for cleaning your scraping tools and for rinsing the piece of furniture occasionally as the work progresses.

As the reader may have inferred, I do not especially enjoy using prepared remover, but when veneered or inlay-

---

*New England red filler for refinishing furniture is fairly easy to mix according to J. Frederick Kelly, authority on Connecticut colonial architecture. The pigment to be used is Spanish brown, a natural earth oxide of a brownish-red color that has been mined in Spain for centuries and widely used by Americans all through the colonial period.

Mr. Kelly's directions as published in *Old Time New England* for October, 1943, are: "Mix the pigment with enough raw linseed oil to make a thin, creamy paste, and allow to soak for several days. Then add, for each pound of pigment, one ounce of brown japan drier, and add enough turpentine to make a quart. Stir thoroughly before using, and from time to time during use as the pigment is heavy and inclined to settle in the thin vehicle."

This Spanish brown is not as widely used as formerly and can only be obtained from dealers handling a wide variety of painter's supplies but the results justify the trouble envolved. Substituting either Venetian or Indian red for it will not result in the same shade and tone.

decorated furniture must be stripped, I know of no other method. For pieces made of solid wood, I prefer the one painters have followed for years—that is, remove the old finish by burning. Use a small gasoline torch to "fry" the old finish so that it can be peeled off readily with a putty knife. It is not difficult to learn how to handle one of these torches, and if one works carefully old paint or varnish can be removed without scorching or charring the wood beneath.

If you have never used such a torch, practice on a piece of discarded furniture until you have learned the knack of working with one. If possible, get the smallest size—one-pint capacity. Larger sizes are heavy and hard to handle. Use either benzine or untreated gasoline for fuel. Never use automobile gasoline. Its "anti-knock" ingredient fouls the torch burner and extinguishes the flame. By sweeping the surface of the piece a little at a time with the flame, paint or varnish will soften and begin to bubble about like syrup dropped on a hot griddle.

As soon as this occurs, move immediately to the next spot. Otherwise, the heat will char the wood. When a fair-sized area has been so treated, remove the burned coating with a putty knife or scraper. Stubborn spots may need to be touched again with the flame, but this should be done cautiously, lest the surrounding wood be scorched. A safer way is to attack such spots with a well-sharpened scraper.

In using a burning torch, don't apply the flame directly to a glued joint. Its heat can quickly bake the life out of the glue and loosen the joint. Also, keep it away from direct contact with hinges or other bits of metal. The latter absorbs the heat much faster than wood, and either a warped hinge or scorched wood can result. One more don't—*never* use a burning torch on wood carving, fine reeding or delicate moldings. Clean these with liquid remover and a small stiff-bristled brush, and pick off stubborn bits of finish with a chisel or knife blade.

Having cleared away the old finish, either with remover or torch, the next step is to make all surfaces smooth. This also rids them of any traces of old finish that may remain. A good scraper is needed for such work. Most hardware stores sell small block scrapers with replaceable blades. These have just enough curve so that the ends of the blade do not gouge into the wood. I have found such tools much easier to use than the older pieces of saw steel. Also, when a blade becomes dull it can be replaced quickly.

In scraping, do not dig in and rip off ribbons of wood. With them go all the mellowness of age. Scrape lightly, and remember that some woods are softer than others. When all surfaces seem to be reasonably smooth, the scraper can be laid aside in favor of either sandpaper or bats of steel wool. Whichever is used, have an ample supply, ranging from slightly coarse to the finest. I have found that excellent results can be achieved with a combination of both, alternating as the immediate situation requires. Use coarser grades sparingly for the rough spots, then shift to the finer ones, and finish with 0000 sandpaper or grade zero steel wool.

When all surfaces feel satin-smooth, the piece is ready for its new finish. Shellac is used for pieces in the natural color of wood; paint, when New England red filler, old Amish blue of Pennsylvania Dutch provenance, or the dull bottle green of old Windsors is to be simulated. Here it should be stated emphatically that one of the chief secrets of a smooth surface is several thin coats.

For either shellac or paint, have the solution thin enough so that it flows readily from the brush. Orange shellac is used for most furniture finished in the natural color, but white shellac is best for maple or other light-colored woods. Add a quarter as much alcohol by volume to the shellac, so that its consistency is about that of thin salad oil. Dust the piece thoroughly, as well as the place where the work is to be done, before starting to apply the shellac. Be sure your brush is clean, free from loose bristles and absolutely dry. A brush two to three inches wide is about right for most furniture. With even, straight strokes, all in the same direction, apply the shellac so it spreads evenly and none of it remains standing on the surface.

For good results, work quickly. When finished, let the piece dry for a day; then give it a light sanding with 0000 paper to remove any traces of brush strokes. Repeat for at least three coats. Five may be needed if the pores of the wood require that many before they are thoroughly closed. Be sure to follow each coat with light sanding, and add more alcohol if the shellac thickens even slightly. After the final coat is dry, the sandpaper should be moistened with kerosene or other very light oil. This reduces its cutting capacity, so that this last sanding is in the nature of a gentle buffing. Apply no pressure. The oil-moistened sandpaper should practically glide over the surface. Then wipe the piece thoroughly to remove every trace of oil, and a satin-like finish now emerges.

For a paint instead of a shellac finish, the work proceeds in much the same way. After the paint has been mixed and tried out for correctness of shade *on an old piece of wood,* not on new lumber or cardboard, be sure it is thin enough so it will flow easily and spread evenly. If too thick add turpentine, about a tablespoonful at a time, until the consistency is right. With a clean dry brush, using the same straight parallel strokes, apply the first coat. Let it dry thoroughly. Remember paint is much slower in drying than shellac. Give this first coat the same light sanding with 0000 paper and follow with at least two more coats, each carefully sanded. Finish with the oil-moistened sandpaper and the result will be a silky-smooth surface with no noticeable gloss. If a high gloss, approaching that of an automobile body, is wanted (but I advise against it), it can be achieved by a single coat of clear spar varnish kept nearly as thin as the paint.

Sometimes, with painted furniture, such as a stenciled

Hitchcock chair or Boston rocker, after the decorative detail has been retouched the entire surface may be given a coat or two of thin white shellac or clear spar varnish. This preserves the original finish and does not change the color tones beneath it. Here again, each coat should be sanded lightly.

After such refinishing, a light coat of wax does no harm to any piece of antique furniture. It is hardly necessary to go to the extreme of painting the wax on, removing the excess and then polishing. Enough wax for this purpose is still on cloths already used for the process described earlier. What is important is to take time enough and rub hard enough so that this very slight film of wax will be evenly distributed.

CHAPTER X

Making Drawers Track and Beds Usable

One of the most common causes of frayed tempers and caustic remarks about "broken-down antiques" from non-collecting members of a family has to do with drawers in old case pieces that stick and won't track. This is a common failing. Through years of use, drawer sides and runners become worn. When this occurs, the drawer bottom is prone to rub. Not only does this part fail to work smoothly, but a fine wood dust is generated that gives rise to a snap diagnosis of "termites" on the part of the layman.

Practically never is this diagnosis correct. The rubbing of the drawer bottom is what produces the powder-like dust, not wood-boring insects. Repairing drawers so they will work smoothly is one form of restoration that even the most orthodox collector will agree is necessary, especially if a piece is to be used. Fortunately it is a relatively simple repair that can be done by the collector.

The runners on which the drawers move back and forth are in most pieces simply strips of wood glued and nailed to the sides of the case. Sometimes they are fitted into grooves as well. In either case, it is usually possible to remove the runners and reset them with the worn side down. If this is carefully done, even the old nails can be saved and used again. But since the average home workshop is not usually provided with the proper clamps for use in regluing runners, it will be easier to use screws instead of nails. Two or three in each runner are enough in most cases. The old nail holes should be bored slightly smaller than the size of the screw. After putting glue on the runner and on the case, simply fasten the runner tight to the case with the screws. Number eight or number ten screws are heavy enough and should not be more than half an inch longer, including the head, than the runner is wide.

Furniture made with paneled ends had the drawer runners nailed to the outer uprights, front and back. Guide strips were glued on top of these. When runners are reversed, the guides too, which also suffered wear, should be removed and reversed.

Many tables and stands are found with the drawer runners tenoned into both the front and back of the frame. Runners of this type are difficult to remove, so the most practical method is to glue a strip on top of the old runners after they have been planed smooth. Strips of wood cut to

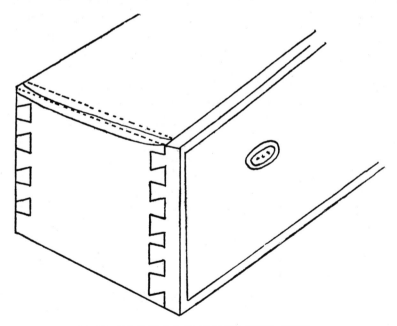

HOW TO REPAIR WORN DRAWER SIDES
Dotted lines indicate new strip set in to replace wood worn away through years of use.

fit the worn grooves are not satisfactory for a permanent repair.

Some chests of drawers have a width of board, the entire depth from front to rear of the case, inserted beneath each drawer space. Such boards are generally known as dust partitions. Because the grain of the wood in this partition ran at right angles to that of the wood in the drawer sides, the wear was mostly at the front edge where the drawers rocked. If the strip which is added to build up the drawer sides is made wider than the groove worn in the dust partition, nothing will have to be done about filling in this groove.

Building up the lower edges of a drawer is simple enough if the wear has not extended into the slot which holds the drawer bottom in place. Draw a line across the drawer side at the lowest part of the wear. Plane the side smooth to this line and glue on a strip of the correct size. Nails should not be used unless they can be countersunk at least a full quarter of an inch. The added strip may be of any kind of wood, but it makes a better appearance if it is the same as the wood in the drawer side. Hardwood strips make a long-wearing and easy-sliding drawer. For planing drawer sides, there is an inexpensive little bull-nose plane which is very convenient for this purpose.

It is sometimes possible to make a quick and fairly satisfactory repair by gluing a strip to the bottom of a drawer next to the worn side. After a drawer has been built up, the added strips should not be planed down so far that the drawer touches the case at any other point than on the runners. Careful attention to this detail will prevent chipping of veneered fronts, or damage to delicately inlaid edges or other forms of drawer-front trim.

A drawer should also be fitted with a small block on the back of the slide to prevent it from going into the case too far. Drawers with a lip, or overlapping edge, should have this stop placed in such a position as to allow a small fraction of space between the lip edge and the front of the case. Many chests have this stop placed on the front strip that separates the drawer openings, but from a purely practical angle this is not always a good feature. Drawer bottoms sag and, as the drawer sides wear down, drag on these stops.

Oftentimes drawer bottoms shrink, and as they are held at the back with nails they pull out of the slot in the front of the drawer. Many times it is possible to remove the nails and slide the bottom forward without having to add an extra strip to fill in the shrinkage. This should be done before building up the drawer sides. Where a slight shrinkage has caused the dovetailed edges of a drawer to loosen, they should not be repaired by driving in nails. Glue the sides of the drawer just as they are, and then fill up the shrinkage with wooden wedges also well glued.

If drawer sides and runner are kept soaped or waxed, their operation will be greatly improved and a large amount of wear prevented.

Despite the many unhappy results seen, an old four-post bed is one of the easiest of household furniture to restore. One must first be sure, however, that the bed in question is worth it. Even if the collector does the work himself, time and energy count for something and, if it is to be handed over to an experienced cabinetmaker, common sense demands that one weigh the cost against the piece's intrinsic worth.

So let the problem of restoration start with buying. Be sure all parts of the bed started out together. The old frames were originally designed to be taken apart—upright posts, headboard, side and cross rails. It frequently happens that through the years one part or another has been mislaid or lost. A missing part can, of course, be replaced; but the bed then ceases to be all original. The wisest course is to buy such a bed only after you have seen it assembled. If it is of the tall type, be sure the parts of the canopy frame are all present. Inspect details of head and foot posts to make sure they were originally made for the same bed.

Chisel numbering on these, as well as on side and cross rails, will tell the story. These chisel-made Roman numerals should all be of one size and have the characteristics of one person's handwriting. Make sure that the posts have not been shortened at either top or bottom. Converting high-posters into low ones by cutting off the posts just above the level of the headboard, and making low-posters still lower by cutting off six or eight inches from the feet, were common practices from about 1850, when the modern bedstead came into fashion.

On the other hand, one need not be concerned if the various parts are not of the same wood. Except for very fine and sophisticated examples, several kinds of wood may have been used. Pine or white wood were favorites for headboards. Nor were the rails always of the same wood as the posts. Numberless combinations are found, such as maple posts and oak rails; cherry posts and rails of maple; even pine posts and hardwood rails were sometimes used. The old cabinet-makers took what they had on hand, since the simpler beds were either finished with paint or stain, except when the posts were of the finer hardwoods, such as mahogany, walnut, cherry or fancy-grained maple.

Assuming, then, that you have acquired a bed in fair condition, the work of restoration follows. For obvious reasons, a thorough cleaning is in order. Working out of doors because of the fire hazard, go over the parts liberally with gasoline. Use a wide brush for the flat surfaces and a small round one for mortises and rope holes. Gasoline is not only a practical insecticide, but much dirt and grime can be removed by wiping the parts with clean rags while still damp.

The next stage is making necessary repairs, such as gluing a split headboard, filling shrinkage cracks in posts and making minor repairs to the turnings, and so on. Then comes the problem of making the frame firm and rigid. Fine old beds were provided with eight screws that passed through the upright posts into the ends of the rails, where they engaged nuts, inserted and concealed by wooden plugs. The simpler beds depended for rigidity on the rope network that not only held side and cross rails firm but served as a primitive spring for the tick of straw, corn husks or feathers. Very ingenious and charming, but we have become too soft for such rigors. Even the most ardent antiquarian would reach for a modern spring and mattress after a night spent on such an instrument of the Inquisition.

If the bed is without bolts, an excellent solution is to make the head and foot permanent units and then insert bed bolts to make these two sections fast to the side rails when turned tight. To make headposts, headboard and upper cross rail one, the headboard should be wedged and glued into its mortises at the same time that the cross rail is being made fast. Then tightly fitting dowels must be driven into holes already bored through the posts, so that they will pass through the tenons of the rail that fit into the mortises cut in the posts. The same process holds for the two footposts and the connecting cross rail. Unless you have the long gluing clamps, it is advisable to have this work done by a cabinetmaker. He has the proper tools, without which it is practically impossible to do a satisfactory job.

Inserting the bed bolts and countersinking the nuts is also no work for the inexperienced. The entire bed must be assembled. Then with an auger slightly larger than the diameter of the bolts, holes are bored through the four posts and four or five inches into the ends of the side rails. Their location should be along a line that is the vertical center of the posts and at the same time approximately equidistant from the top and bottom of the side rails. Then a mortise is cut on the inner side of each end of the two side rails, so that the bolts may be in a position to engage the nuts when inserted in the holes bored for them. When the bolts have been turned tight, the mortises are concealed by filling them with plugs covered with glue and driven home with a hammer.

Now the bed is ready for finishing. If it is a fine hardwood, a shellac finish that will enhance the beauty of its grain and color is, of course, the most desirable. With the more ordinary woods, one has a choice. If the original finish of either New England red filler or Amish blue paint is more or less intact, it should be preserved. If all traces of original finish have been lost, the owner can follow his own inclinations. The bed can be scraped and sandpapered and then finished in the natural with several coats of shellac. If either the red or blue-green of the original finish is desired, it can be accomplished by carefully mixing paints until just the right shade is achieved. Then two thin coats, with light sandpapering after each coat is thoroughly dry, will give an even, smooth finish.

The bed is now ready for the spring. Don't try to manage with one of stock size—they practically never fit. The most satisfactory way is to order one made according to the dimensions of the bed. It should be from an inch to an inch and a half shorter than the length of the bed, measured from the inside edges of the rails, and the same amount narrower than the width, again measuring from the inside.

There are two methods of supporting the spring. Angle irons made for the purpose can be bought and screwed onto the side rails, or two cross slats can be attached to the underside of the rails. Whichever method is followed, the spring when in place should not stand over half an inch higher than the upper surface of the rails. Then when the mattress is put in position, it will rest evenly on rails and spring.

These are the steps in getting an old bed ready for modern living. Here are a few don'ts. The early beds are admittedly shorter than the modern bedsteads. If you insist on standard length, don't try splicing the side rails. Put them away in store closet or attic and have new ones made. Then, if at some future time you wish to sell the piece, you have a bed with original parts and value nowise lessened because for a time extra long side rails associated with it. The same holds if you have a field bed and find your ceiling too low to accomodate the fine sweeping curve of its canopy. Have a flat canopy made if you will, but put the original away in a safe place.

The biggest don't of all concerns the baneful practice of cutting over old beds for twin size. Not only is their value as antiques practically destroyed, but even the late, low-priced varieties look out of scale. The old craftsmen had an eye for line and proportion. When either is tampered with, the result is unhappy, to say the least. Moreover, the cost of mutilating these old beds is frequently more than that of good reproductions.

CHAPTER XI

Fixing Tables and Chairs

Of all problems in antique furniture restoration, tables present about the severest tax on the skill, ingenuity and patience of the repairer. For everyday use, the top and leaves of a table must be smooth, reasonably level and free from cracks and splits. Yet one or two centuries of use frequently take their toll in concave, convex or twisted warping, as the case may be. This is the natural result of gradual drying of the wood; and the wider the boards used in leaves and top, the more pronounced the warp.

In addition, there may be splits which follow the grain of wood, but as long as the board in question has not broken in two, it can be repaired with shims so that leaf or top remains a single piece of lumber. Also, with those originally fabricated of two or more boards, the glued joints often come apart and need regluing.

Variations of these ailments occur with the double-top card table, where the upper part has warped so that it no longer lies flat on the lower one when closed, and also with tables of the tripod base type where the top has cracked or warped. Barring abnormal conditions, the following course of treatment should prove beneficial to ailing tables, large and small.

The prime requisite in such restoration is patience. Nothing extraordinary in the matter of tools is necessary. The usual complement of cabinetmaker's clamps, big and little, fine chisels, saws and a glue pot are sufficient. But a table top or its accompanying leaves that have been gradually warping over the years cannot be made true and straight in a day, or even a week; it may take a month or two. If you attempt to put them at once under enough pressure to reduce curl or twist rapidly, nine times out of ten they will crack and split. The proper method is a gradual increase of pressure each day, until the upward or downward curl or twist has been overcome. Then acting according to judgment, go the other way ever so slightly, so that when released from pressure the wood may react to a slight degree and the final outcome be the desired trueness.

But you must realize that sometimes the idiosyncrasies of the grain of the wood are such that, though you try everything possible, the warp or twist cannot be corrected. Ex-

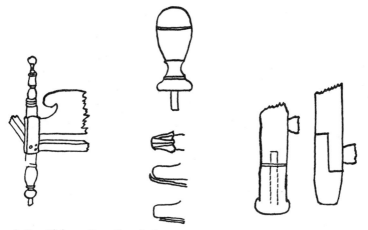

Left: *Fixing a Four Post Bed*
Drawing shows where new bed screw should be located, also places for the two dowel pins that hold the cross rail beneath head board fast.

Upper Center: *A Replacement Finial.*
Dowel in base is inserted in hole bored in top of upright.

Center: *Ways to Tighten Loose Chair Stretchers.*
At top wrap with cloth soaked in hot glue; at center a thin splint of wood inserted before stretcher is returned to its position; at bottom a thin wooden wedge is driven beneath stretcher without removing it from socket.

Lower Right: *Two Ways to Lengthen Cut-off Chair Legs.*
At left, turned replacement attached with dowel that extends well up into original leg. At right, by a lap joint with dowel inserted horizontally.

perienced cabinetmakers know this, and when confronted
by such unruly wood they recognize it as "wild grain" and
admit their inability to cope with such conditions.

Assuming a normal condition, the procedure is relatively
simple for taking out warping that has resulted in a convex
or concave curl, or a combination of both, best described as
twist. Begin by dampening the leaves or table top, so that
the wood will give under pressure and not split. This is done
by removing the boards from the table frame and placing
them on a bed of thoroughly moistened excelsior with the
unfinished raw wood surface down, in order that the pores
can absorb as much moisture as possible. Place heavy weights
on them so that the straightening process will start as soon
as the wood begins to react from the dampness. Leave them
there until they begin to show that the dampness has penetrated into the fiber of the wood. If necessary, sprinkle the excelsior with a little additional water.

Next, put leaves or top under positive pressure. The best
apparatus for this is a press in which a screw like that of a
builder's jack provides the pressure. Lacking such a press, you
can simulate one with four large cabinetmaker's clamps and
sections of old bed rails a little longer than the width of the
warped part. Place these rails under and above to form a crib-
bing and apply pressure by tightening the screws of the hand
clamps.

Neither press nor clamps should be turned too tight at
first. Just be sure positive pressure is being exerted and then
leave things alone for twenty-four to forty-eight hours, after
which the screws should be tightened a turn or two. This
should be repeated regularly until the warped part is absolutely true. Knowing just how much force to apply at a time
is a fine point learned only by experience. One sign of over-
zeal is the slight noise of rending wood fiber. If this is heard,
immediately release the pressure by a quarter or half turn.

After the parts have been pressed sufficiently, leave them

in position about a week, or until all moisture absorbed from the bed of damp excelsior has disappeared. They are apt to revert to their previous warped state if taken out of the press before thoroughly dry. The hotter and drier the room where the press stands, the better, for it then becomes to all intents and purposes a drying kiln, such as is used in lumber mills to season new material.

As soon as a table top has been removed from pressure, it should be replaced on its framework with all speed. Plug old screw holes with soft wood, and using sharp new screws, of the same length as the original ones, turn them as tight as possible. The top may not fit tightly to the bed and some of the screws may have to be given additional turns for several days before this can be accomplished; but when this has been done, if the old screws have been saved, remove the new ones, one at a time, and replace them with the old ones.

In rehanging the table leaves, the old hinges, if usable, ought to be straightened. Also, the old screw holes for the hinges should be plugged with pine or other clear, soft wood. Finally, the leaves should be put in place and the table left standing for a week or more in a warm, dry place.

Do not view with alarm a slight upward curl in the leaves even after all this treatment. It is characteristic of a genuine antique table and is to be expected. The wider the leaves, the more noticeable the curl. Unless very pronounced, it is not a fault but a distinct proof of genuineness.

In replacing tops of large tables, with or without leaves, or those of the small light-stand type, whether with four legs or tripod base, never glue the top to the table frame or cross piece or pieces that attach it to the tripod shaft. Such gluing eliminates give and take between top and base. Through changes of temperature and drying, it may result in the top splitting—something that will not occur if only screws are used.

So much for correcting warping. The other major repair is that of regluing where top or leaves were originally of two or more pieces of wood. Begin by washing thoroughly with hot soap and water the surfaces to be reglued, until all traces of old glue are eradicated. Do not plane the edges. Such tight joining is not characteristic of an antique. Instead, use the best quality of cabinetmaker's glue. Apply it as hot as possible and put the parts together as they were originally. Clamp them tightly, at the same time using lengths of bed rails to forestall convex or concave curling or twisting. Allow plenty of time for the glued joining to become thoroughly dry.

If the condition of the edges is such that added strength is needed, cut corresponding mortises into the edges in three or four places, according to length, and make tenons to fit into them tightly. Glue and clamp as before, being sure that each mortise is as thoroughly moistened with glue as are the edges themselves. In this way the glue joint will have added strength, with little likelihood of coming apart for many years.

To bring a double-top card table back to normal, put a strip of wood about half an inch thick between the two leaves, not further back from the front edge than the center. Then with a pair of wooden hand clamps, bring the upper leaf under pressure. Increase this slightly every other day until the top leaf is true. Then allow the table to stand for several days before releasing.

Chairs have probably suffered more damage from wear, abuse and mutilation than any other group of household gear. This is particularly true of slat-backs and other turned chairs. Legs cut off, finials damaged or lost, slats broken, arms snapped and stretchers missing or broken are a few of the casualties such chairs have suffered. Some of the damages are difficult to repair, in the sense that much time and care are needed to do a proper job. For this reason, it is best to make sure before buying a chair in need of repair that it is a sufficiently good type to warrant the trouble.

Minor injuries resulting from normal wear are best left untouched. These add to the interest of a piece and are proof of age. Cut legs, however, may be restored without harming the originality of the piece. Broken frames of chairs not worth fixing make the best repair parts. These can be bought quite reasonably from dealers who specialize in furniture in the rough. One frame will supply enough parts to repair several chairs.

There are two ways of building up cut legs. One is by the use of a doweled extension; the other, by fastening the extension with a lap joint. When there are no more than two or three inches to be restored, the dowel does not have to be turned on the extension. Simply make a clean cut on the end of the chair post and glue the extension on with hot violin-maker's glue. After allowing the glue to set for a day, drill a three-eighths-inch hole through the extension, and continue about an inch into the chair post. Drive into this hole a maple dowel, first rounding the end a little and putting glue into the hole. Amateur restorers will find that a small back saw will make a clean, easily jointed edge.

The hole through the extension can be drilled before jointing. Use a machine bit rather than a wood twist bit. This same method can be used for attaching turnip feet and other types of turned feet. These, of course, will have to be made by a local wood turner or bought from firms supplying parts for reproductions.

The lap joint is used where the legs have been cut to attach rockers, or where they have been cut off close to the bottom stretchers. Use of a lap joint saves drilling new holes for the bottom stretchers, and also has the advantage of preserving more of the original post.

All extensions should be made slightly larger in diameter than the old post and then worked down with a draw knife, plane or fine wood rasp and sandpaper. Most of the old chair posts were not perfectly round; one side is sometimes flat, so that it is not possible to turn an extension in a lathe that will be an exact fit.

There are several ways of tightening loose stretchers. Each method depends on the condition of the chair and the looseness of the joints. Wedges may be driven into the space between the stretcher and socket. Stretchers that will pull all the way out can be wrapped with a rag soaked in glue and driven in again. A piece of splint oak from an old chair seat makes a good wedge to use where the stretcher is loose enough to pull out. The oak is soaked in glue, bent over the end of the stretcher and then driven into the socket. Where there is a large amount of space between the stretcher and the socket, the hole is sometimes filled with a plastic composition and the stretcher carefully forced back into the socket. These compounds have a tendency to shrink, which makes this method a less permanent job than one done by using wood wedges. Never nail a stretcher.

Ends of arms that are broken or stretchers of a fine design can be saved by doweling a piece on, in the same way as suggested for leg extensions.

Finials that need replacement will have to be turned by a local wood turner. They should be made exact in size, with a quarter-inch dowel attached that need not be over one inch long. Wherever possible, the joint should come where one of the old scorings appears on the chair upright.

A slat that has to be replaced should be made of an old one, whenever possible. It is rather difficult for the average home restorer to bend a straight piece of old wood into a suitable curve. The broad band of an old spinning wheel, if of hickory, makes good slats. An old bed rail of maple is usually thick enough to cut a curved slat from on a band saw. When slats are so cut, saw marks can be removed by scraping.

Examination of an old chair will show that most of the slats are pinned as well as wedged into the socket. The wedges will be found usually on the under side. Pins are made of hickory and are whittled out and not turned, as is a dowel. The irregularities of such pins help make a tight joint when they are driven in, and this makes it difficult to disturb such a joining. Don't do it unless unavoidable.

Of all the antique slat-backs that I have acquired at one time or another, only one of them has ever come to me with seat intact. Replaced seats in no way detract from the original condition of antique chairs. No chair that has been in use around a home from three to five generations could be expected to retain the seat provided by its maker, unless it were a Windsor or other wooden-seated type.

Whether of rush, splint, cane or upholstery, a chair seat that is used at all has a life of about twenty-five years. So the collector can expect to reseat almost every old chair he adds to his collection. On most of them, if he has time and patience, he can do the work himself. The time to do it is, in most instances, just after the framework has been repaired and refinished.

The four types of seats mentioned above and their names indicate the material used. With none is the work complicated. Patience and ability to follow directions are the two requisites. The best and clearest instructions for doing such reseating are to be found in a set of four ten-cent pamphlets issued by the Home Extension Service of the Department of Home Economics, Cornell University, Ithaca, New York. Each pamphlet is complete with clear diagrams that explain every step in the work, and for those who want to do their own reseating, I recommend that they start by getting these pamphlets and then follow the directions therein.

Here I wish to add just one injunction. Do not use the modern twisted paper substitute for the old rush. Coming, as it does, in coils like heavy package cord, it is somewhat easier to handle than genuine rush, but a seat made of it is an anachronism on an antique chair. It is all right for the modern factory-made product, in which this twisted paper is consistently used to hasten production and cut costs, but it ruins the appearance of one made by the old cabinetmakers.

CHAPTER XII

Proper Hardware for Antique Furniture

With antique furniture, the most frequent and most readily rectified cause of depressed value is incorrect hardware. Both dealers and collectors have long recognized that an important secretary or chest of drawers, complete with its original brasses, is easily worth a quarter to a third more than if it lacks them.

But fine pieces of this sort, with drawer pulls and keyhole escutcheons all present or accounted for, are not found every day. The majority, when discovered in the rough, either lack original hardware entirely or, at best, have but a part of it. The condition may range all the way from a bail or two being missing to all escutcheons gone except perhaps one.

Some thirty years ago, replacing missing hardware of this sort was a serious problem. It was a case of robbing Peter to pay Paul—that is, having found a fine old piece with brasses missing wholly or in part, one then had to look for another of the same period with brasses intact, but sufficiently inferior in line, craftsmanship or condition to warrant removing its hardware for use on the better piece. Even then one's troubles were not over. Often, in brasses of the same type, the handles might vary enough to make the transfer impossible without plugging the old holes and boring new ones. Granted that this was the best that could be done, it was far from ideal, for the plugged holes as well as the new ones left traces that plainly showed what had been done, and to a degree lessened value.

Happily this trial-and-error system is no longer necessary. A number of brass founders now make a specialty of providing missing parts and have also developed adequate assortments of typical period brasses. These are faithful copies of old ones and are as fine reproductions as it is humanly possible to accomplish. So there is no excuse today for either collector or dealer having a piece of furniture with brasses at variance with its period. Yet all too common are some ill-mated combinations as a William and Mary secretary with Sheraton rosette knobs; a Chippendale chest of drawers with pulls of the Hepplewhite period in every detail of their shape and ornamentation.

Sometimes the error is not so obvious. The brasses may be of the period, but not enough care has been taken in securing the right size; so new holes have been bored and, from the inside, the drawer fronts are distinctly marred. For the discriminating, at least, the piece has been lessened in value. Yet a little care in selecting reproduction or replacement brasses of the exact size to fit the original holes was all that was needed.

Assuming that a piece of furniture has its old brasses, but the carcass needs repairing or refinishing, the first step, obviously, is to remove the hardware and carefully put it away in a safe place. In a perfect world, no escutcheon would break while being removed nor would any bail wander away from its fellows and be lost while waiting its return to the secretary or chest under repair. Things being as they are, however, either or both sometimes happen but the damage is not irrepairable. With a perfect one as a pattern, it is easy and comparatively inexpensive to have a new part specially made. Then when the piece of furniture is ready for its brasses, the presence of one or two elements in the set which are replacements goes unnoticed, and, in the end, such steps classify as justifiable repairs.

Even with pieces that lack their original brasses, through carelessness of former owners or through time and use, it is by no means difficult to determine what they were and select reproductions that fit, in both period and dimensions. The old cabinet brasses mirrored the various periods as distinctly as the furniture they adorned.

To cover this briefly—the seventeenth-century oak chests and cupboards had simple wooden knobs, usually about twice as long as their diameter. Such drawer pulls were also used on early eighteenth-century tables, cupboards and like pieces of Pennsylvania Dutch provenance. These handles should never be confused with the much larger turned wooden knobs of the mushroom sort that came in the late Sheraton and American Empire years.

In the William and Mary period, the drawer pulls were of the tear-drop pattern, and plates and keyhole escutcheons were either circular or square and set on the diagonal. These were sometimes used in the Queen Anne period, but more frequently the handles were small bails with plates behind them like those used for the keyholes, in outline something akin to a conventionalized bird with outspread wings. This pattern was much elaborated in the Chippendale period, and such brasses are well known under the general name of "willow brasses." Sometimes they were plain and sometimes of an intricate cut-out design.

During this period bail handles were also used, with small rosettes immediately behind the posts that held the bails in position. In this design the keyhole as well was usually a rosette. The Hepplewhite period brought a distinct break in the design of brasses. These were square, oval or octagon, with bail handles and plates decorated with a wide range of stamped designs. When the Sheraton style succeeded this, the rosette knob, with either geometric or floral motif, became the fashion. This continued through the American Empire years, with wooden and glass knobs becoming a characteristic of the period.

With these types of brasses in mind, it will be possible

in practically all instances where a piece of furniture has lost its original hardware to discover traces that indicate the kind and sort it had when new. A single surviving escutcheon, or a handle plate, hidden beneath succeeding layers of varnish and paint, should be sought for and eagerly salvaged. Such a survivor provides unquestionable evidence, and new handles should be as nearly like it as possible. If even this is missing, inspect the drawer fronts carefully in strong sunlight. The old hardware usually left scars and scratches that can be seen on the old varnished surface, and they provide a valuable key to the outline and size of reproduction brasses proper to use.

But if succeeding generations have tried to bring the old piece up to date, so that all evidence of its original fittings has been destroyed, there is but one thing to be done. Knowing the type and period of the particular piece, secure reproduction hardware for it that has been made to conform. If in doubt, consult museum collections and illustrations in books and magazines until a corresponding piece has been located. Make careful observations of its brasses and secure reproductions of the same design. In doing this, one last caution should be observed. Be sure that the new brasses are of the same size, so that boring new holes in the drawer fronts may be obviated.

CHAPTER XIII

Remedies for Ailing and Damaged Glass

From its nature, glass would seem less amenable to repair than any of the other collectibles that interest antiques enthusiasts. A piece either is in prime condition or it is damaged. If the latter, the general impression is that little or nothing can be done to remedy even minor defects.

Yet there is at least one example of a piece literally broken into a thousand fragments being skillfully repaired. The Portland Vase, that most famous example of ancient cameo glass, was, as everyone knows, broken by a maniac about a hundred years ago and subsequently so reassembled and mended that scarcely a trace of the outrage is visible today. This was, of course, a priceless piece, and the need of preserving an example of what had long been a lost art was great enough to warrant corresponding expense.

Granted that few, if any, of us have much chance of owning a Portland Vase, and that it is advisable to let the broken glass in a collection remain in that condition or discard it, there are often certain minor defects in an otherwise fine piece of glass that can be minimized. Of course, to accomplish this requires skill and a wide variety of glass working tools. Such repairs are not for the amateur, but must be done by a professional with a properly equipped shop. What a good glass repairer can accomplish in eradicating blemishes caused by time and use is almost incredible. With grinding and polishing wheels he can remove all traces of nicks and chips.

Take, for instance, a goblet, wine glass or flip glass marred by a slight nick on the rim. Skillful grinding and subsequent polishing will cause this to disappear entirely.

The same repairman can also regrind a glass lamp base that is not in first-class condition because careless handling through the years has resulted in slight chips along the lower edge. The same can be done with a piece of lacy Sandwich or pattern glass.

Closely related to this work is a repair possible with decanters. Sometimes a stopper of the same type and period as the bottle does not fit properly. If it is too large, the repair is relatively simple. The base of the stopper can be ground smoothly and evenly until it fits the neck of the bottle. Even the opening of the latter can be slightly enlarged by grinding. If the base of the stopper is too small, a sleeve of glass must be applied and then ground so that a firm fit may be insured. This repair is naturally not as successful, for it is always obvious.

In fitting decanters with replacement stoppers, be sure that they match in tint. In the case of Irish glass, for instance, that made in the Waterford district had its particular cast of color, a slightly smoky, bluish tint; that from Cork, a straw or amber tone. These fine differences in tone are only apparent to the average observer by close comparison; but if a stopper from Cork were to be fitted to a decanter that originated in the Waterford section, this slight difference in tint would immediately be emphasized and the original purpose defeated.

In grinding and polishing glass to remove slight chips and nicks, one should be sure that the piece so treated is rare and fine enough to warrant the expense of restoration. There is also the off chance that the piece may break or crack in the process. For example, a Stiegel-type sugar bowl has a very slight chip on the finial of the cover, and is therefore not in perfect condition. Shall the owner run the remote chance of the cover breaking during the process of having this small blemish ground and polished away, or shall he "bear the ills he has?" It all depends on the temperament of the owner. The chances of the cover coming through in perfect condition with blemish completely smoothed away are probably ninety-nine out of a hundred. He must be prepared for the one ill chance, however, even at the hands of a glass grinder of skill and long experience, and accept it, should it happen, as a contingency incident to the work.

Sometimes a piece of old glass is quite free from nicks or chips but the surface has begun to disintegrate, giving a slightly cloudy or frosted appearance. If it has gone beyond the initial stages it is an example of sick glass, and such it must remain. There are two causes for sick glass. Either the proportions of the batch from which the piece was made were incorrect, or the piece has oxidized from chemical reaction. The latter may have been due to the glass having been left for years in a damp cellar, having been buried in the earth, or having been used overlong as a container for some liquid.

Extreme examples of sick glass are sometimes very beautiful, such as the irridescent pieces recovered from Egyptian, Grecian, Roman or other ruins of the early civilizations of the Mediterranean. It was these delicate colorings that the late Louis Comfort Tiffany sought to accomplish in his favrile glass by the addition of various minerals.

If all sick glass resembled Mr. Tiffany's favrile productions, it would present no problem. Unhappily, there is seldom any irridescence, but only a cloudy, frosted tone, making the piece look sick indeed. In the initial stages, this condition can be rectified by repolishing, provided both sides of the piece can be reached. The surface is thus cleared of the damaging cloudiness. Plates, bowls, drinking glasses and similar shaped pieces lend themselves to this treatment. If the disintegration is only on the surface and has not permeated the material, such work is usually permanent. Otherwise, it is of only temporary benefit and the telltale cloudiness shortly reappears.

Old flasks and bottles, even with a mild attack of this

malady, cannot, because of their shape, be sent to the re-polisher, since he has no means of reaching the inner surface of the glass with his bluffing and polishing wheels. On the other hand, some collectors have developed an ingenious technique for treating bottles so afflicted, and it is reasonably successful. Take a pliable green twig, and attach a swab to one end. Dip it in a good grade of clear, colorless mineral oil and patiently work it around inside of the bottle. Rub each cloudy spot until it disappears under the action of the oil. A bottle or flask so treated must then be tightly corked and kept so, because the cloudiness will return as soon as the oil has evaporated. I have seen flasks that have been given this oil treatment and remained clear for upwards of five years, even though kept on a shelf in a window and thus exposed to a maximum of sunlight.

This treatment is, of course, only a palliative and not a cure. Sometimes, too, the oil finally gives the glass a slightly yellow cast. A problem not in the nature of a repair or re-storation but one which often faces the bottle collector, is that of cleaning pieces disfigured with a dried sediment. If this does not respond to thorough and liberal doses of good soap and water, fill the bottle with either a mild acid or alka-line solution, and let it stand for a day or two. It may be necessary to use first one and then the other. If the sediment is of an acid nature, the alkaline solution will produce a chemical reaction that will loosen it; if the substance is alkaline, the acid solution will have the desired effect. In no case should a powerful reagent be used. Vinegar and washing soda, both inexpensive and mild, are excellent reagents.

If sediment still remains, there is a further course of action. Fill the bottle about a quarter full of clear water and add about two tablespoons of fine *steel* shot. Cork the bottle and shake it thoroughly. This scours the inside effectively. If shot is not available, clean bird gravel used with less water can be substituted. *Never use lead shot.* It is not sharp enough to be effective, and besides if there is any trace of chemical in the bottle the result may be a coating of lead solution. This is not only difficult to remove but, in extreme cases, can practically ruin the bottle or flask.

Another good method of removing stubborn sediment is to fill the bottle with a strong solution of lye and cold water. Let it stand for two days. Paint, wine dregs or vinegar stains will soften and can then be removed with a brush or the usual quantity of steel shot. If the outside of the bottle is also stained, use the same solution for cleaning that, and finish by washing the entire bottle in soap and water. Brilliant, sparkling glass should result. This method is used by one of the foremost collectors of American glass bottles and flasks in this country.

CHAPTER XIV

Care and Treatment of Old Prints

There are two points of view in regard to the care of old prints. One is, never do anything to them. The other is that careful treatment is necessary for their preservation and restoration. The latter is obviously sensible when the work only involves removing surface dust and the incidental dirt that a print may have acquired through the years, especially if tacked on the wall of a harness room or elsewhere, unprotected by glass.

There is also a divergence of opinion about the rust-colored marks caused by knot holes or cracks between boards in the thin wood used as backing of a frame. Some believe that these marks will spread after the cause has been removed by proper framing. Others believe that proper framing will stop the action of such marks. If they actually do spread and cause further damage to a print, then they should be removed and the print restored.

These rust-colored marks cannot be removed successfully by any easy home methods. Prints, especially valuable ones, should be turned over to experts for such work. The chemicals used are such that, unless employed by experienced hands, they may cause irreparable damage. Practically all good print shops can arrange to have this work done satisfactorily. No print, regardless of condition, should ever be discarded without first consulting a reputable print expert about its value and the possibilities of restoration.

A print with an evenly mellowed surface, even though much duller than it was originally, is in collectible condition. Any attempts to brighten its colors would be useless and would add nothing to its value. Valuable prints are fastened to cardboard by using hinges, similar to those used in mounting stamps. On large folios, three or four hinges are necessary on the small ones, two or preferably three. These hinges can be made of any kind of gummed cloth tape, but it is better to use a glue that will not stick too tight and tear the print if they need to be removed. One inch or more wide for small folios, and two or more inches wide for large folios are the best sizes for the hinges. The outside ones should be flush with the edges of the print. This prevents torn corners. Hinges are, of course, fastened to the back of prints.

The cardboard on which the print is mounted is two inches or more larger in each dimension than the print itself. It is a good idea also to cover the print with a piece of transparent paper similar to cellophane. This paper is glued to the cardboard all around its edges and allows the print to be seen and handled without danger of injury, and keeps out dust and air.

There are some print cabinets that have drop fronts and the prints are filed in upright position. For prints kept in such a cabinet, the method of mounting just outlined is almost mandatory. Desirable cabinets can somtimes be acquired at auction sales of store fixtures. I have even seen some made of old pine feed boxes. These, when cleaned and finished, fitted very well with other antique furnishings. Old spool boxes, such as were used in country stores, are suited to small folio prints.

Surface dust and grime can be removed from prints quite easily by anyone. It is accomplished by going over the print with what is known as a "kneaded" eraser. The strokes should be light, and care should be exercised so that none of the descriptive lettering or coloring is removed. I have heard of such practices as covering a print with cornstarch and putting it in strong sunlight, but the eraser method is conceded to be the best and safest way to clean off surface grime. A very dirty margin can be whitened by rubbing lightly with powdered pumice, but this should never be done to any part except the blank margins.

Aside from these suggestions, there is little that the collector can do to correct damages that have occurred through the years. However, there is much that can be done to prevent further deterioration. Stains and foxing, if not too pronounced, can sometimes be removed or rendered less prominent by careful use of a bleaching compound. Such "washing" should be done very cautiously, for it can damage colors and even rot the paper. Ordinary laundry solutions such as javel water or clorox will do this cleaning, but they should be well diluted, and an inexperienced collector should not attempt such cleaning on a print of value. Have the work done by a professional who knows when to stop, rather than run the risk of ruining the print by overdoing the washing.

Slight tears on the margins of prints can be repaired by backing them with other paper. For this, it is best to use photographic mounting tissue and to cut the patches as small as possible. Do not use library paste, as it wrinkles the paper when it dries.

With a print on which the margins have been trimmed for framing or other reason, the only thing to do is to have it carefully matted by a good picture framer. If the margins have been only partially removed and the title is still attached, such damage is not too great, but is always to be regretted.

Prints that are to be hung on the wall require a different mounting than those kept in file cabinets. Most of the damages already mentioned are the result of improper framing, which allowed dust and air to reach the print. Valuable prints that are to be hung on the wall should be as nearly dust-proof and air-proof as possible. The best method is to make an airtight unit of glass, print and backboard.

A strong piece of cardboard, preferably not wood-pulp paper, is laid flat. On this is placed the print, then the mat, if one is to be used, and finally the glass. The edges are fastened together and sealed by using passe partout binding or similar tape. This complete unit is placed in the frame. Another backboard of cardboard is added, and then over this is placed the customary wood backing. The latter can be omitted if heavy enough cardboard is used for the second piece of backing. After the backboard is tacked in, a piece of strong manila paper is glued to the frame but not the backboard. About every five years the glued paper and tape should be examined to see if they need replacing. This method of framing gives almost perfect protection for any print.

Margins of prints should not be cut to fit a frame. Have the frame made the exact size of the print including the margins. The only time margins are trimmed is when they are badly dog-eared. Even then, it would be better to repair the margins by using transparent tape and filling in the holes with bits of old paper from a worthless print. It is the usual practice to have the width of the margin at sides and top the same. The bottom, which has the descriptive printing, is somewhat wider. This printing should not be covered by the frame or mat, if one is used.

The ideal way to keep unframed prints is in a cabinet with drawers large enough to allow any size of print to lie flat. For complete protection from air, dust and handling, these prints are mounted in hinged folders of heavy cardboard. Sometimes the tops of the folders are cut out like a mat to show the print. In other cases, the print is mounted on heavy cardboard and a piece of strong manila paper glued on to make a cover. Even the least valuable of prints should not be filed away without some sort of protection between each print, such as a sheet of tissue paper placed over the face of each one.

Prints should never be kept rolled. When one is acquired in this condition, the best way to take out the curl is to place it face down on a table, weight it with books, heavy boards or a slab of marble and leave it for several days. In doing this, work cautiously, since sometimes the paper is brittle and will crack if not handled gently.

CHAPTER XV

Care of Pewter, Silver and China

In the restoration and repair of antiques of all kinds, from furniture to china, silver, pewter and so forth, the idea that if a little is good a lot is better has no place. Instead, the collector, and especially the enthusiastic beginner, should be as ardent an adherent to small doses, well spaced, as was the old-fashioned homeopathic family doctor. Also do not put too much faith in that ingenious tinker-like repair man you have been told about who can do anything from making new legs for a highboy to welding broken glass.

Although I know an automobile mechanic who has more ability in making old clock movements run and keep time than any man I have ever met, except for a few European-trained clockmakers, my experience has been that most of these "fix-anything" handy men are apt to do the wrong thing when turned loose on an antique. Their intentions are the best in the world, but through lack of appreciation of antiques they are liable to commit such atrocities as replacing the handles of a silver tray with rivets instead of resoldering them—to cite a true but extreme example. These handy men are often engaging characters, and charge much less than experienced workmen who are specialists in their fields, but the results of their ministrations can be near to tragic. So if you take an antique to one of them, stay with it and supervise what is done.

There still remain a few simple and practical things that the collector can do for himself in restoring and caring for the pewter, silver and china that he may collect. These will be set forth in this concluding chapter.

First, there is pewter. One of the collectors of my acquaintance prides himself on the fact that he personally has re-conditioned almost every piece in his collection that needed such attention. The room in which he does this is as replete with equipment and special tools as a dentist's laboratory. In fact, as he sits here cleaning and polishing a teapot and forgetting the daily problems of his business in New York, his long white smock and professional manner give him a somewhat clinical appearance. What this man can do for an ailing pewter plate, porringer or coffeepot is amazing. He has spent ten years, at least, teaching himself the art of pewter restoring, and guards the finer points of it as closely as a professional magician does his best tricks and illusions.

There are a few fundamentals, however, which this pewter specialist and others like him employ in reconditioning the pewter that passes through their hands. With many pewter pieces, the collector is chiefly concerned about cleaning and polishing. This he can do if patience and strength of arm hold out. He would do well to start with simple tasks and practice on pieces made by American pewterers of the "coffeepot" era. These are fairly plentiful, and not too valuable. If, at first, through main strength and awkwardness he injures such a piece, he can charge it off to tuition.

If early in his pewter collecting he acquires an earlier and rarer piece, he should entrust its repair and reconditioning to an expert. When it comes back, he can examine it closely to see how well the work was done, and this will give him a standard for his own efforts.

In starting to clean and polish a piece of pewter, hold it to the light and examine it for any fine holes. If it is a tankard, teapot or other hollow piece, fill it with water to test for leaking seams or joints. These can be repaired with the deft use of a small electric iron, such as is used for radio repair work, and plumber's solder. Here, again, practice is needed to learn how to use the least possible amount of solder in closing a hole or sealing a seam.

Next comes cleaning and polishing. Unless a piece is badly oxidized, the dull slate-gray surface of a long neglected piece will yield to patient rubbing with a mild abrasive. I have found that an ordinary kitchen scouring powder, moistened with a little kerosene, is satisfactory. With stubborn pieces, I try powdered Bristol brick, standard for scouring steel knives in the kitchens of our grandmothers. If this doesn't produce desired results, try the fine grade of emery called "flower of emery" in hardware stores, and then fine steel wool. With either, use kerosene instead of water. It brings out the desired sheen more readily. Even with this procedure, some stubborn spots may have to be rubbed with a piece of fine emery cloth. This should be done sparingly or one will cut too deep into the metal. Such cleaning and polishing must be followed by thorough washing with soap and hot water to rid the pewter of all traces of oil.

Some pieces that will not come bright under this treatment because the oxidation is deep-seated may yield to sterner methods. Try soaking such a piece in a penetrating oil used at garages to loosen rust-frozen bolts. While still covered with the oil, scrub the piece with a piece of shingle end or other handy fragment of wood. If scales still cling to the surface, add a little nitric acid and scrub again.

If this also fails, the last resort is boiling in lye; but in using this remember that lye is a strong caustic and can cause a serious burn. Wear goggles to protect your eyes from a chance spatter, as well as oil-treated leather work gloves for the safety of your hands. Have a pair of kitchen tongs at hand so you can remove the piece for examination. Since the fumes of boiling lye are disagreeable, if not harmful, the window should be open and it would be wise to have a bottle of vinegar at hand as a counteragent if the lye should spatter.

Do this boiling in an iron, brass or enamel-ware kettle,

never in one of aluminum, for the lye will eat through that metal. Do not use too strong a solution; a half-cup of lye to a quart of water is strong enough. Watch the boiling carefully. Boiling too long can ruin a piece of pewter, so remove the piece frequently for examination and stop the process before the caustic action has gone beneath the surface.

Pewter so treated should be thoroughly rinsed or even soaked in clear water to remove all trace of lye. Then the piece is ready for ordinary polishing.

Once a collection of pewter has been cleaned and polished, the problem is how to keep it bright and shining. If the pieces are used on the dining table fairly regularly, ordinary washing with soap and water, together with occasional polishings with any good silver polish, will be sufficient. With pieces not used frequently, the best practice is to polish them about twice a month. Rubbing them with a woolen cloth dampened with a light oil will be sufficient. In order not to leave fingerprints that cause tarnish, wear a pair of fabric gloves when doing this polishing.

There is not much the collector can do with brass or copper antiques besides cleaning and polishing them. If there is a break or a soldered joint has loosened in andirons or candlesticks, I have found it better to have it rectified by a repairman who has an acetylene torch welding outfit. With bronze braising rods and the high heat of his torch, there is hardly any repair such a man cannot accomplish. When the work is finished and excess metal has been ground off with an emery wheel and the piece then buffed smooth, it is difficult to see where the repair has been made. Leaking seams or small holes in brass or copper teakettles are also better repaired in this manner. It also holds true for the open kettles that are coated with block tin on the inside, but these should be touched with solder which is the nearest thing to block tin generally available.

For polishing brass and copper antiques, there are a number of compounds that can be bought at hardware stores. These will produce a fine polish with plenty of rubbing, but the best of them are fairly expensive. For a cheaper polishing agent, salt and vinegar has been used for a very long time. Even less costly is the sweat, sand and water method. If you live in the country and happen to have an ant hill handy, dig out some of the very fine sand with a kitchen spoon. Then with some old cloths and a little water added to the sand, keep working on the pieces until they gleam. I saw this treatment applied to a set of old fireplace tools with finials so black that they resembled the wrought iron of the tools themselves. Within an hour of patient work, the soft sheen of brass gleamed as though these fireplace tools had been given regular care for years. Sea sand sifted through a fine coffee strainer to remove any particles of grit is equally good, and probably easier to get. Most building supply yards carry it as part of their line of plasterers' supplies. Twenty-five cents' worth of this sand will be more than enough to polish a large collection of old brass and copper.

In order to eliminate repolishing, some people like to have their brass and copper pieces coated with metal lacquer. This should never be done with andirons or kettles intended to be used near or over a fire. Intense heat will burn the lacquer and discolor it, after which it can only be removed by polishing on a power-driven buffing wheel.

Repairs on antique silver are difficult. Making them calls for such special tools that the collector should not attempt to do the work himself. If possible, select a professional who has had experience with antique pieces and has a reputation for doing fine work. Such a repairman will not mar a piece, nor hurt it by smearing on too much silver solder. Good workmen of this type charge well for their work but the results justify it. Be sure, however, when you take a piece to be repaired that it is understood that you do *not* want it burnished. If this is done, it will lose all of its patina and look as if it were new.

There are a number of excellent prepared polishes for cleaning silver, and if directions are followed good results can be obtained. Occasionally a piece that has been put away for a long time will become so tarnished that it looks practically black and ordinary polishes will not clean it. On such pieces, silversmiths use a special chemical dip. It is poisonous and most collectors prefer to have such work done for them, but for those who want to do their own dipping, here is the recipe of the dip my grandfather, B.M.Bailey, used all the years that he was an active silversmith in Vermont and for many years afterward to keep his own silver gleaming.

He kept it in a tightly covered five-gallon stoneware crock with "POISON" in two-inch red letters painted on side and lid. Into this crock he put two gallons of rain water and a pound each of cyanide of potassium and "salts of tartar," as potassium nitrate was then called. This was stirred with a wooden stick until the chemicals were completely dissolved. When using the solution, he had a large tub of scalding hot water standing close beside the dipping crock. Each piece of silver was dipped by hand, and as soon as the tarnish had disappeared it was thoroughly rinsed in the hot water. After the silver had been wiped dry. it was rubbed vigorously with a rouged chamois skin to remove any slight grayish tinge that might remain from the dipping. A crockful of this dip will retain its potency for many years, but having one in the home is not recommended unless the container is adequately labeled and kept under lock and key when not in actual use.

For the collector whose antique silver is kept in a cabinet or enclosed cupboard or, if flatware, in a drawer, the frequency with which it must be repolished can be materially reduced if small cakes of camphor are put with it. Camphor fumes keep silver from tarnishing. One small cake is enough for a good-size drawerful of flat pieces, and two cakes to each shelf of a cabinet or cupboard should be adequate to keep the larger pieces displayed there bright for some weeks.

China, next to glass, is the most breakable of all antiques. Therefore the collector will be more frequently faced with the problem of repairing broken or damaged pieces of china than anything else. Although in magazines appealing to hobbiests some very alluring advertisements can be found of supplies with which the collector can do expert work as his own china-mender. I have yet to see any sizable amount of home-done repairs of this sort that are as satisfactory as those done by expert china repairers.

Such men can do very fine work, which comes as near as possible to remedying perfectly an unfortunate break. To my mind, when a piece of china must be repaired, I think it is worth paying the price to have it done by one of these experts. They can rivet broken plates, mend and re-attach snapped handles, patch broken teapot spouts, make knobs on covers fast with small metal bolts, rebuild missing fingers on figurines and do other remarkable repairs that cannot be seen unless a piece is inspected very carefully. Sometimes such repairs are visible only with the aid of a magnifying glass.

For pieces of either porcelain or earthenware that have become discolored with tea or food stains, there is a simple and harmless way for removing most of such stains. Simply soak the piece in clorox or a strong solution of bleaching powder, now used in many industrial processes. The glaze of such a stained piece is slightly porous, and soaking it for a day or two in either solution will permeate beneath the glaze and bleach the stains.

Recently I made some tests to see how effective such bleaching could be, and here are some of the results. An

English porcelain teacup having a pronounced brown line along its age crack was soaked overnight and the brown line disappeared. It has not returned, although the cup has been used for coffee at least once a week since then. A small teapot, probably of English ironstone ware, although unmarked, was covered with a network of fine brown hairlines. After it had been soaked in the clorox solution for several days, all the stain disappeared except for a few traces at the tip of the spout, and even they were much fainter.

In the case of a Leeds platter that was covered with mottled light brown stains, I poured paraffin over half of it and when the paraffin was cold, filled the platter with the bleaching compound. Two days later I emptied it and removed the paraffin. The unprotected half was practically clear of stain, while the other retained its brown mottling.

As further checks to be sure this soaking in a bleaching solution would not have any bad effects on decorations done in colors or gilt, especially those applied over the body glaze, I put a number of different pieces into the bleaching bath and left them for several days. The pieces included an Oriental Lowestoft blue and white cup, a piece of French porcelain with a heavy band of gilt, a Staffordshire transfer-ware saucer in sepia and a small vase with decorations in five colors. I examined each closely and found the bleach had had no effect on the colors of any of the pieces. Also some broken pieces put through the same test showed the solution had not reacted on the material itself, even at the cross section of the break.

As a result of these tests, I feel that use of such a bleaching bath to remove food and other stains is a safe and practical means of restoring stained pieces of both porcelain and earthenware to their original tone. Such stains may return in time, but if that happens the pieces can be put in another bath for a second bleaching.

Just one last observation. If you have antique china vases, figurines or the like, don't have them converted into electric lamps if this requires drilling them. Such conversion damages their value as antiques, and usually they are not much good as a source of artifical illumination, which is the true purpose of lamps. Leave such antiques alone, and enjoy them as colorful and interesting decorative accessories.

Some outstanding American old houses fully furnished with appropriate antique furniture and decorative accessories are now maintained as museums and opened to collectors who wish to visit them and see a wide variety of antiques in appropriate surroundings. Among them are:

Alabama
Mobile: Fort Conde-Charlotte House
Connecticut
Farmington: Hill-Stead Museum
Hartford: State House
Litchfield: Tapping Reeve Law School
Madison: Nathienal Allis House
Norwich: Leffingwell Inn
Mystic: Marine Historical Museum
New Haven: New Haven Colony
   Historical Society
Stamford: Headquarters House
Waterbury: Mattatuck Historical
   Society
District of Columbia
D of C: The White House
Delaware
Wilmington: Old Town Hall
Florida
Palm Beach: Whitehall Mansion
Sarasota: John Ringling Residence
Georgia
Savannah: Davenport House
Illinois
Galesburg: Carl Sandburg Birthplace
Kansas
Abilene: Eisenhower House
Kentucky
Danville: Mc Doewel House and
   Apothecary Shop
Frankfort: Liberty Hall
Massachusetts
Boston: Harrison Gray Otis House
Deerfield: Old Deerfield, Individual,
   houses and museum
Nantucket: The Oldest House
Stockbridge: Stockbridge Mission House
Michigan
Dearborn: Greenfield Village
Mississippi

Natchez: Stanton Hall
Saint Louis: Tower Grove House
Vicksburg: Historic Camden Hearth
North Carolina
Halifax: Royal White Hart Masonic
   Lodge and other Houses of Historic
   Halifax
Winston-Salem: Old Salem
New Hampshire
Portsmouth: The Capt. Nutter House
New Jersey
Allaire: The Deserted Village
Madison: Washington Headquarters
Middletown: Marlpit Hall
Trenton: William Trent House
Trenton: Old Barracks
New York
Albany: Schuyler Mansion
Bedford: John Jay House
Cooperstown: Fennimore House
Croton-on-Hudson: Van Cortland
   Manor
Garrison: Boscobel Restoration
Hyde Park: The Vanderbilt Mansion
Hyde Park: Franklin Delano Roosevelt
   Home
Kingston: State House
Kinderhook: Kinderhook House
Lawrence: Roch Hall
Monroe: Smith's Cove Village
Oyster Bay: Rayhan Hall
New York City: Hamilton Grange
New York City: Jumel Mansion
New York City: Theodore Roosevelt
   Birthplace
New York City: The Old Merchant's
   House (Tredwell House) 29 E. 4th St.
Oyster Bay: Sagamore Hill, Theodore
   Roosevelt Residence
Quogue: Old Schoolhouse

Rochester: George Eastman House
Tarrytown: Sleepy Hollow Restorations
  on the Tappen Zee
Tarrytown: Sunnyside
Yonkers: Philpse Manor Hall
Ohio
Cincinnati: The Taft Mansion
Newark: Sherwood-Davidson House
Troy: Hart and Cluett Family Mansion
Pennsylvania
Lancaster: Wheatland, James
  Buchanan Residence
Lancaster: Historic Rock Ford
Philadelphia: Powell House
Rhode Island:
North Kingston: Gilbert Stuart

Birthplace
Providence: Carrington House
Wisconsin
Portage: Old Indian Agency House
Madison: Ole Bull Residence
Vermont
Middlebury: The Sheldon Art Museum
Weston: Farrar-Mansur House
Virginia
Charlottesville: Monticello, Thomas
  Jefferson Home
Fredericksburg: Kenmore House
Mount Vernon: George Washington
  Home
Richmond: John Marshall House
Williamsburg: Colonial Williamsburg